True
Self-Esteem

True Self-Esteem

Precious in the Eyes of God

JIM McMANUS C.Ss.R.

Liguori/Triumph

LIGUORI, MISSOURI

Imprimi Potest:
Thomas D. Picton, C.Ss.R.
Provincial, Denver Province
The Redemptorists

Published by Liguori/Triumph
An imprint of Liguori Publications
Liguori, Missouri
www.liguori.org

Previously published in 2004 as *The Inside Job: A Spirituality of True Self-Esteem* by Redemptorist Publications, Chawton, England.

Library of Congress Cataloging-in-Publication Data

McManus, Jim, 1938–
    [Inside job]
    True self-esteem : precious in the eyes of God / Jim McManus, C.Ss.R.—
1st U.S. ed.
        p. cm.
    Originally published: The inside job : a spirituality of true self-esteem. Chawton, Hampshire, England : Redemptorist Publications, 2004.
    ISBN 0-7648-1280-7 (pbk.)
    1. Self-esteem—Religious aspects—Christianity. I. Title.

BV4598.24.M36 2005
233'.5—dc22   2005040843

The editor and publisher gratefully acknowledge permission to reprint/reproduce copyrighted works granted by the publishers/sources listed on page 158.

Liguori Publications, a nonprofit corporation, is an apostolate of the Redemptorists. To learn more about the Redemptorists, visit *Redemptorists.com.*

Printed in the United States of America
09 08 07 06 05   5 4 3 2 1
First U.S. edition 2005

For my niece Emer

Contents

Contents

Foreword

When Jim McManus first invited me to get involved in this project, I had a rather mixed reaction.

Yes! There is a real need for a book that does just what this book sets out to do. The need for a spiritual dimension to self-esteem is very widely acknowledged; and, yet, efforts to explain what that means, or what it might involve, are rare. I knew of none. Jim's book set out to fill this gap, and I was enthusiastic, delighted by his invitation to contribute to that project.

But self-esteem is a psychological concept, rooted in our very human natures. Would this project be able to honor that fact? Would it be able to "take the science seriously," while at the same time providing a nourishing Christian view of spirituality and self-esteem? I confess that, as both a Catholic and a scientist, I was concerned.

I need not have worried. Jim's power as a spiritual writer is well established and strong as ever. His openness to science is truly impressive, particularly his ability to take onboard the products of research and blend them with spiritual insights.

The whole issue of the "self" is an area where psychology and theology continue to conduct intense exploration, but they traditionally use concepts that have no obvious way of connecting the two disciplines to each other. What this book presents is a new synthesis between these two approaches, which brings out the way that our psychological natures relate to and form the basis for our spiritual selves, and, conversely, the way that our spiritual selves enliven and enrich our human lives.

Whether you are already a believer in a "higher power" or not, this book, through its twin roots in psychology and faith, has something to offer every believer.

I wish you every joy in reading it.

DR. STEPHANIE THORNTON
CPSYCHOL, AFBPsS
DECEMBER 2003

Preface

For the past thirty years, I have been involved in the healing ministry. I have had the privilege of ministering to hundreds of people on a one-to-one basis and of conducting workshops and inner-healing retreats in many parts of the world. My approach to this ministry has been shaped and determined by one conviction, namely that much of the inner pain which people carry around is due to what they are doing to themselves. Many people become skilled in the art of self-rejection and self-denigration and, as a consequence, they begin to feel bad about themselves, uncomfortable with themselves. In inner-healing work, I have always encouraged such people to take the road to freedom. This is the way of unconditional self-acceptance and self-love.

Self-acceptance, however, can be either grudging and half-hearted or joyful and grateful. I began to realize this truth as I tried to understand why an individual, after the experience of inner healing, after accepting self, lapsed back into a state of self-rejection. I came to see more clearly that what we need is a spirituality of joyful and grateful self-acceptance, or a spirituality of true self-esteem.

I first heard the phrase "spirituality of true self-esteem" from a colleague of mine, Sean Murray, when I visited him in his retreat center in California. As we shared experiences about the ministry of inner healing, he said that what was most needed today was a new emphasis in spirituality. He developed his ideas for a spirituality of true self-esteem.

I began conducting retreats and workshops on this theme in 2000. I turned for help to two close friends, Marie Hogg, who had collaborated with me on inner-healing retreats for many years, and Sister Germaine O'Neill, who had recently returned from her years of teaching and lecturing in Kenya. I want to acknowledge my indebtedness to them. I learned a great deal by listening to them develop aspects of our theme during our retreats.

I asked Redemptorist Publications, my British publisher, if they would consider publishing a book on the spirituality of true self-esteem. Before making a decision they commissioned a leading research psychologist, Dr. Stephanie Thornton, who had been head of the Psychological Department of Sussex University, to undertake research on the subject. Her findings convinced the editors that there is a real place in the market for a book that offers a solid spiritual basis for that much-sought-after value which is good self-esteem. The U.S. edition of this work is being published by Liguori Publications, another publisher of the worldwide Redemptorist publishing houses.

Stephanie very kindly continued to collaborate with me on the contribution that good psychology could make to spirituality. We edited the final text of this book together. I acknowledge her substantial contribution to the development of the book, especially in the areas of the integration of psychology and spirituality.

Three professors of theology read the manuscript and made very helpful suggestions. My thanks to professors Hamish Swanston, Jack Mahoney, S.J., and Raphael Gallagher, C.Ss.R. I was also greatly helped by the suggestions which Dr. Julie Rutkowska made when she read an earlier draft of the manuscript. My sincere thanks to her.

I also want to thank my editors at Redemptorist Publications for their help and encouragement in writing this book.

My thanks, too, to the hundreds of women and men who have followed my retreats on the Spirituality of True Self-Esteem over the years. Their enthusiastic response to the message of these retreats was very reassuring to me in the work of preparing this material for publication.

Finally, I want to thank my Redemptorist brothers in the community at St. Mary's, Kinnoull, and Mrs. Anne MacDougall, the secretary of our Center of Spirituality. Without their constant support and collaboration, none of the retreats that I have conducted on the theme of this book would have been possible.

True
Self-Esteem

1

Why a Book on the Spirituality of Self-Esteem?

*Not to know what the world is to be
ignorant of where you are.
Not to know why it's here is to be
ignorant of who you are.
And what it is.
Not to know any of this is to be
ignorant of why you're here.
And what are we to make of anyone
who (doesn't) know where or who they are?*

<small>MARCUS AURELIUS, EMPEROR OF ROME</small>

Good self-esteem is as necessary for a life of happiness as the air we breathe is necessary for life itself. People from a wide variety of backgrounds, starting from many different assumptions, would agree with that sentiment. Bookstores offer shelves of texts on how to develop self-esteem, and courses designed to build your self-esteem abound.

One striking thing about these self-help books and courses is that, whatever their differences of approach and style, virtually all agree that self-esteem *must* have a spiritual dimension. If you want good self-esteem, you had better develop your spiritual side! Equally striking, these books and courses typically offer little or no advice as to how this is to be done, or even what your "spiritual side" may be.

For example, I recently read the lectures given by an educational psychologist to teachers in London on raising the self-esteem of pupils. He had a whole section on spirituality without one suggestion on how to live it. Telling people that they are spiritual beings without sharing with them some insights about living spiritually is as frustrating as telling them that they have a million dollars in a bank account without giving them an access code. "Figure it out for yourself" is not a sufficient follow-up to the confident assertion that we are spiritual beings.

What Is Spirituality?

At one level, each of us has some sort of intuition about what we mean by spirituality. And yet, this concept is elusive. There is no one universally accepted, clear, and satisfying definition. We may yearn for a deeper spirituality, but many of us remain confused as to exactly what that might mean.

However deeply one may experience spirituality in one's own life, expressing what that means in a way that another person can understand is difficult. Perhaps the best way to come at this problem is through analogies and examples. Let me share with you a discussion I had with Stephanie Thornton, a psychologist, on how to expand on this issue.

For psychologists, there have long been two different ways of describing human beings: as physical, biological entities, with bones, muscles, blood, nerves, and the like; and as psychological entities, with feelings, thoughts, and ways of behaving. Of course, the feelings, thoughts, and behavior that a person may have will always have some sort of physiological dimension: I require arms to hug a needy child, and I cannot propel those arms without muscles to direct the bones and flesh, or without nerves to instruct the muscles. But the electrical and chemical processes that direct the hug exist at a very different level from the empathy and care that I experience in *wanting* to hug that child, or in deciding to reach out to do it. It is as if a human being (or any other part of our world) exists at many different levels, levels that coexist and interact, but are not the same.

Stephanie used this analogy, in describing the many levels at which our world exists and can be described:

Take this mug. At one level, one could describe it in terms of the atoms that compose it, atoms that vibrate and interact with one another in ways that only physics can describe. And that is a true description of what it is, a bunch of atoms, structured in a particular way. Everything in the physical world can be described that way. At another level, it is a mug: an object with functions and purposes, capacities and incapacities. Its function and purpose is to hold food, food that is liquid rather than solid. This level of description places this object squarely in a particular practical relationship to me: its character as a mug determines its behavior, and how I can use it. This, too, is a true description of what the thing is, although it is a description at a very different level, with very different implications from the description in terms of atoms. But there is a third level at which I can describe this particular mug: it is the one my son bought me on a particular sailing holiday. It is what he bought me the very first time when, at age nine, he was skilled enough to sail a dinghy alone across a wide lake to another town and go shopping. At this level of description, the mug takes on a very special individuality: it becomes a symbolic object, carrying special meanings, significances, and feelings that far transcend its existence either as a bunch of atoms, or as a mere mug. It is at this level, and this level alone, that the individuality of this particular mug matters, or that the existence of this particular mug enriches my life. It is at this level of awareness that the things that make life worth living exist. And yet, the mug exists, and can be truthfully and usefully described, at all three of these levels, at one and the same time.

Like this mug, human beings exist at many different levels. We too are composed of atoms—that is, physical structures. In other words, we are made of physical bodies. We too have functions and purposes that determine our behavior. Unlike mugs, we also have thoughts and feelings about these functions, purposes, and behaviors. This is our psychology, our mind. And just like that humble mug, we too may have symbolic value and significance that transcend either our material existence or our practical function. We may carry a powerful meaning. At this third level the search for our spiritual self points to the search for our own meaning and significance.

Do We Really Need a Spiritual Side?

All the great religions, of course, have always argued that spirituality is essential to our being. This is no surprise, since most of these great faiths start out from a belief in God and in our significance and meaning as deriving from God rather than from the material world. What is surprising is that, in our time, science is also beginning to take the view that spirituality is essential. Increasingly the evidence from science, from medicine, and from psychology is that we do indeed need, and markedly benefit from developing, a spiritual life.

Scientific views about the role of spirituality are changing. For example, Andrew Newberg and Eugene D'Aquili write:

> Until 1994...the American Psychiatric Association officially classified "strong religious belief" as a mental disorder. New data however, indicates that religious beliefs and practices can improve mental and emotional health in several significant ways. For example, research shows that rates of drug abuse, alcoholism, divorce, and suicide are much lower among religious individuals than among the population at large. It also seems clear that people who practice religion are much less likely to suffer from depression and anxiety than the population at large, and that they recover more quickly when they do. Other experiments have linked specific religious activities to positive psychological results; spiritual practices such as meditation, prayer, or participation in devotional services, have been shown to reduce feelings of anxiety and depression significantly, boost self-esteem, improve the quality of interpersonal relationships, and generate a more positive outlook on life.[1]

Evidence of the beneficial effects of spiritual practice is mounting. For example, Elizabeth McSherry has researched the effect of pastoral care on patients in hospitals. She discovered that

> Major open-heart surgery patients who received special daily chaplain visits averaged an impressive two-day decrease in length of stay, compared with their counterparts who did not receive specialized pastoral intervention. And

the patients receiving extra pastoral care also suffered less post-surgery depression, a finding which has great potential significance, given what we have discovered about the relationship between depression and coronary artery disease.[2]

Indeed, medical researchers in America have been amassing evidence over the past twenty years on the healing power of intercessory prayer. Herbert Benson, a professor of medicine at Harvard University, recently published a book entitled *Timeless Healing*, in which he develops the thesis that the human being is "hard wired for God" and that intercessory prayer has a healing effect in sickness. For the past thirty years, Dr. Benson has been working at the interface between medicine and spirituality; between medical treatment and intercessory prayer. And he can write, with refreshing simplicity and humility:

> My patients have taught me a great deal about the opportunities that emerge when artificial barriers are broken down, and how physical ailments inspire soul-searching and a revival of meaningful living, and about how the human spirit enlivens and transforms the body.[3]

In this new atmosphere, Larry Dossey reports that courses on the role of religious devotion and prayer in healing are currently being taught in approximately fifty U.S. medical schools. "This is a historic event, a stunning reversal of the exclusion of these factors from medical education for the most of the twentieth century."[4] Would it not be a supreme irony if doctors in the future felt more comfortable than priests and lay ministers in praying for healing? How many priests would feel at ease preaching what Dr. Harold Koenig of Duke University Medical Center teaches, namely: "Lack of religious involvement has an effect on mortality that is equivalent to forty years of smoking one pack of cigarettes per day."[5]

In Britain, too, there is increasing interest in the role of spirituality in healing. In 2001, a team of scientists in Aberdeen University received funding from the Scottish Executive to investigate the claims of "spiritual healing." Dr. Arrun Sharma, the director of the project, reports that spiritual healing is now sufficiently established as to warrant the kind of serious scrutiny applied to other forms of complementary healing.[6] This is an important acknowledgment that those who undertake the medical care of the community should no longer ignore the spiritual dimension.

Thus the scientific world of medicine and psychology is now beginning to take the spiritual seriously. Increasingly, it is accepted that the human person is a unity of body, mind, and spirit. We cannot split this unity and treat these things as separate. Increasingly we are moving to a more holistic approach, addressing the person at every level. And, in fact, there is no competition between the physical, mental, and spiritual: all three levels of existence are essential and necessary aspects of the person. The message coming from science today is that spirituality is good for your physical and psychological health and welfare.

Of course, this conclusion accords well with our personal insights. Spiritual strength involves a clear sense of the meaning and value of life. Albert Einstein wrote, "The man who regards his life as meaningless is not merely unhappy but hardly fit for life,"[7] a sentiment with which few of us would disagree. The psychiatrist Viktor Frankl, in his classic book *The Unheard Cry for Meaning*, echoes this thought: "Other things being equal, those most apt to survive [the Nazi concentration] camps were those oriented…toward a meaning to be fulfilled by them in the future."[8]

Science and the Nature of Spirituality

It is worth noting, here, that scientific research does not seek to determine what spirituality is, nor can it illuminate the nature of any connection between spirituality and a higher power, such as the Christian God. Science cannot "prove" the existence of God. But what it can do is to study the consequences of adopting a spiritual practice, or making an act of faith in a higher power. According to scientific evidence, these things have a greatly beneficial effect. As Harold Koenig has said, when releasing the results of his research into the relationship between religious faith and the immune system: "We're not trying to prove that there is a higher power. But maybe believing in that higher power could be an important key to people's health."[9]

This research points to a crucial point about spirituality and religious faith: it is important not to confuse the mere practice of a religion with real spirituality. It is quite possible to practice a religion without internalizing any of the values and beliefs of that religion or achieving any real gain at a spiritual level. In such a case, "spirituality" becomes something one puts on and off to suit other needs—for example, the need for social status, self-justification, security, sociability, and so on. Someone in this position may "have religion," but "religion does not have them." Such a person is like those who attend church every Sunday but give no thought to Christian values in their everyday life or in their reflections on themselves. This is the mere shadow of a real spirituality. For the powerfully spiritual, religion holds the meaning of existence. These individuals have internalized their beliefs. Their faith is the deepest thing about them. All their ultimate securities and their very reason for living are found in their faith.

This distinction between those for whom spirituality is powerful and those for whom it is a mere shadow of what it could be is vital. Only powerful spirituality yields health benefits. Dr. Koenig's research team studied the effects of such spirituality on the recovery rates of patients suffering from depression and concluded that, in fact, it is "...one of the most important factors in speed of recovery. The more powerfully spiritual the individual, the faster he or she recovered from depression."[10]

Psychiatrists Scott Richards and Allen Bergin comment:

> It is clear...that these two ways of being religious have different implications for mental health. It is no wonder, then, that generic studies of religion that do not make such distinctions consistently yield ambiguous implications for health because they lump together different individuals under the same label of "religious."[11]

These two psychiatrists emphasize the following points about powerful spirituality (which they call "intrinsic" religious faith):

1. Religious belief gives a person a secure identity that helps the person deal with stress and uncertainties.
2. Religious faith gives a person a real sense of purpose in life and enables the person to find meaning even in death.
3. The positive emotions of faith, hope, and optimism are fostered by ritual and forgiveness and the hope of salvation.
4. Religious belief introduces a person into a network of believers where they have a sense of belonging to the community, a sense of family where they receive social support, and have the opportunity to help others.
5. Religious belief, through prayer and worship, gives the person a sense of communion with God and imparts inner peace.

6. Many religious beliefs call for a lifestyle that includes practicing self-control, taking responsibility, and avoiding destructive or sinful ways.

Science is showing us, then, that some forms of committed religiosity are powerful contributors to our health and well-being. But this message is far from an endorsement of any and every form of belief. Sadly, some forms of religious zeal can even be potent sources of human misery, as is clear from history. Some of the worst atrocities of human history have been perpetrated in the name of religion by religious fanatics.

When we speak about the healing power of religion, we have to be conscious of this dark side of religion. As Scott Richards and Allen Bergin comment: "Although the accumulating evidence for mental and physical health benefits of some features of religiousness and spirituality are massive, we recognize that the picture is not always positive. Clinical practitioners who are treating disturbed individuals often see some of the worst aspects of religion."[12] The strong implication is that we need to think very carefully about the forms of spirituality that we adopt.

How Do I Become Spiritual?

At its root, spirituality reflects our instinctive understanding that we can transcend the material world that mere things, such as money or cars, can never fill our hearts. We have a yearning for something that is beyond the material world of sight, sound, and touch. Our hearts ache for a meaning in life that is not defined simply by what we have or what we do; we long to embrace a purpose for living that is more comprehensive than making a lot of money or having a good time.

Most of us, at some stage in life, ask questions such as *Who am I? What am I doing in this world? What is the meaning or value of my life? Does it matter whether I do one thing or the opposite? When all is said and done, what do I really amount to? What kind of world is this, and what is my position in it? What happens to "me" when I die?* These are the questions that shape the beginnings of spirituality.

We know in our hearts that we are more than what we can earn. We realize that our human dignity is not derived from what we possess. We have an inner affinity with love, justice, truth, mercy, and compassion. These are spiritual values that the heart longs for. They cannot be measured by material standards. They cannot be won by material success. A person's fame or productivity tells us nothing about his or her compassion, nor are the skills of a professional an indication of the degree of love in the heart. Where, then, are we to look for answers to our spiritual questions? How are we to find a satisfying life at the spiritual level?

The great world religions, as expressed in the Christian, Jewish, and Muslim faiths, or in the great Eastern faiths, such as Buddhism, Hinduism, and Sikhism, have always taught their followers how to access the spiritual world. Many of the things these great faiths teach overlap, one with another. But is it necessary to follow a religious faith in order to find fulfilling spiritual answers? And if so, which religious faith should one follow?

Over recent centuries, we in the West have turned away from religion, seeking the answers to our spiritual questions in science or philosophy; in other words, in the world of reason. But science and reason have not provided satisfying answers. To understand *how* a living thing or a universe works or evolves is not the same as understanding *why* it exists in the first place. An object can be complex, and even beautiful, without having any meaning or purpose. Are we, as highly developed sentient creatures, devoid of meaning and purpose?

Dissatisfaction with scientific explanations has led people back toward a search for answers that is more directly focused at the spiritual level, at the level we think of as religious. And increasingly we have turned away from the beliefs of our ancestors and toward Eastern religions or New Age cults. Is there something unique about these approaches to truth? Is there a "right way" to find spirituality? Is one approach better than another?

Asked about where one should look for spiritual enlightenment, the Dalai Lama suggested that Westerners should try Christianity. So many in our culture seek spirituality, but so few try that path. So many see Christianity as irrelevant in the search for spirituality.

Spiritual questions about the meaning of life beset us all. Throughout this book, I will explore these questions, and discuss insights and practices that can help us to address them, whatever our faith or belief, or whether we have any faith at all. But, in addition, I shall present a Christian perspective on the search for spiritual fulfillment. Rest assured, it is not my intention to convert you to Christianity. Your faith (or lack of it) is your own affair and will be respected in these pages. Rather, in sharing my own Christian, and specifically Catholic, beliefs and practices with you, I hope to explain how a rich spirituality can begin, develop, and be nurtured Christian belief. I hope to show that Christianity is a very real option in this search.

Self-Esteem and Spirituality

Look again at the questions that spur us to spirituality: *Who am I? What am I doing in this world? What is the meaning or value of my life? Does it matter whether I do one thing or the opposite? When all is said and done, what do I really amount to? What kind of world is this, and what is my position in it? What happens to "me" when I die?* These questions call not only for a philosophy about the nature of the universe we inhabit but also for a perspective on the self. We can begin to see why spirituality is so central to self-esteem and, conversely, why self-esteem is so central to spirituality.

To have good self-esteem, we must see ourselves as valuable rather than worthless, and our lives as meaningful rather than pointless. Half the battle is won if we can see our world as one in which, in principle, human lives matter and have a meaning and value—as opposed to being no more than the mechanical unfolding of physical or biological processes. Belief in a higher power can provide one framework for such meaning and value, and so provide the foundations for good self-esteem. The first step to self-esteem is accepting that one is valued, that one matters, and that one has meaning within this framework.

But good self-esteem goes beyond this, even in a spiritual context. Each human life has an intrinsic value and meaning, by virtue of being a human life. We are valuable because we are human. But to have good self-esteem as individuals we must also make sense of, and feel good about, our own individuality. My formula for a contented life is this: *Self-knowledge leading to self-acceptance will yield self-esteem.*

- *Who am I?* Do I really know myself? Am I able to identify my strengths and my weaknesses, my virtues and my faults? Do I know myself "warts and all," or do I gloss over certain parts of myself, my feelings, my actions, my potential?
- *What do I amount to?* How happy am I with myself, with the self I know? Am I, as I stand, acceptable to myself? Am I someone I can respect and be proud of?

Notice, in this formula, that good self-esteem is much more than simply feeling good about oneself in spite of what one may be like. It requires, first, a profound honesty, a profound knowledge of the self, and this may take clear reflection. After all, where's the point in feeling good about someone you do not really know? Where's the point in feeling bad about someone whose virtues

13

you have not noticed? And second, it requires that one be able to respect the person one is. And that means examining both yourself and your values: "anything goes" is not a real basis for respect. This, too, may call for reflection: Are you meeting your own standards? Or have you maybe set the wrong standards to judge yourself by?

Notice too that the formula is not *success plus wealth equals self-esteem.* Success and wealth are always relative. There will always be someone who has more money than you and who seems to be more successful. Conversely, there will always be someone who has less money and appears less successful than you are. Comparisons with other people, as a basis for self-esteem, are invidious. Such comparisons tend toward vanity, to what I would call the sin of pride, where one derives one's pride from imagining oneself better than others.

The sin of pride has its roots in judging others and finding them wanting by comparison with oneself. For the vain, humility is failure, abasement, a devaluing of the self. Humble self-esteem is based not in judgment and denigration of others, but in accepting and loving oneself. For the humble, comparisons between people become irrelevant. A self-esteem of this kind does not need riches, nor the praise of others to value and feel good about the self. For such a self-esteem, humility is not self-denigration, rather, it is a recognition of the equality and equal potential of all people. Really, humility just means being "down to earth" (the word *humility* comes from the Latin, *humilitas,* which means "near to the ground").

Finding Better Self-Esteem

How are we to develop good self-esteem? Perhaps the best starting point is to recognize where we are now: to take a good long look at ourselves, consciously to notice what we believe about ourselves, and how we treat information and evidence about ourselves. Truthfully, how do you feel about yourself, and why?

Many of us carry views of ourselves that are wounded to some degree, though we do not always realize it. Often, these wounds began in childhood. Children are enormously vulnerable, enormously dependent on the adults around them for their growth, and even their survival. They need to feel secure in the affections of those on whom they depend. That is to say, they need to feel loved and protected, valued, whatever they may do, whatever may happen. Such security allows the child freedom to explore the world and to learn, uninhibited by the fear of criticism or rejection. Without this secure love, the child's life may be driven by anxiety or even fear, so that the freedom to learn and develop is distorted by the need to avoid criticism and rejection. As Carroll Saussy writes, "Most people who work as counselors would probably agree that the most essential ingredient in adult self-esteem, the foundation of adult self-esteem, is the experience of having been genuinely accepted and cherished as a child."[13]

A self-esteem wounded in childhood can perpetuate lifelong assumptions and strategies that characterize low self-esteem: dismissing signs of worth and value in oneself, seeking out and emphasizing evidence of worthlessness and failure, and avoiding challenges and opportunities to grow and develop one's potential. Anyone can feel down at times, but wounded self-esteem can heal, as I hope we will discover through the rest of this book.

First Steps Toward a Spirituality of Self-Esteem

We are embarking on an exciting journey together, not to faraway exotic lands, but into our own unexplored selves. This inner journey is the most important and most rewarding journey you will ever make. We will journey inward and seek to discover afresh the wonder of our being. As T. S. Eliot said:

> We will never cease to explore
> And the end of all our explorations
> Is to return to where we started
> And see the place for the first time.[14]

No one can build self-esteem or spiritual strength for another person: we each have to do that for ourselves. It will not happen in a flash of inspiration. It takes hard work. How can we start? Too often, the answer we get is "figure it out for yourself." This book aims to help you in that work, by drawing on ancient wisdoms to provide concrete exercises to direct your efforts.

Exercise

Let us begin by centering ourselves, getting ready for the work of discovering ourselves and our spiritual natures more profoundly:

- Choose a time when you have ten minutes or so to spare. Find a quiet place, somewhere as free of interruptions and disruptions as possible. Sit in a comfortable chair, with your spine upright, your two feet firmly on the floor, your arms relaxed by your side. Close your eyes.

- Feel the tension in your feet and ankles. Let that tension go: let your muscles relax and feel the tension flow out from your feet and ankles to the earth. Now focus on your legs and do the same thing. Feel the tension in your muscles, and let it go; relax and let the tension flow out through your legs to the earth. Now do the same thing with your hips, and then your spine, your chest, your arms and hands, your neck. Feel the tension around your jaw, then feel it around your eyes. Let it go...relax. Let it flow away through your body and into the earth.
- Notice your breathing. Do not try to change it. Just listen to the rhythms of your body as you relax.
- Notice the sounds that come from outside and from inside the room. And now go back to paying attention to your breathing.
- Sit quietly like this for a while. What is passing through your mind? Maybe there is nothing there except a stillness. Or maybe you have some thought or image, or some feeling or emotion. Notice what it is and accept it.
- Bring your thoughts back to your breathing and relax.
- And then gradually return to the world.

This technique for deep relaxation may be familiar to you. It is a practice common to many religions, as well as to many non-religious approaches to spiritual questions. It should leave you very calm and very aware of yourself at many different levels: body, mind, spirit. This is an excellent place from which to start our work toward a stronger spirituality and self-esteem. It is also one of the oldest forms of prayer: the oldest form of Christian prayer. Let us call it our "centering" prayer.

2

Healing the Wounded Self

Two men looking through prison bars.
One sees mud, the other sees stars.

TRADITIONAL

Each of us lives by the word of others, though we do not always notice it as such. Recall, for instance, an occasion when you were feeling in great form: everything was going well; you had no worries; the family was well; you had good friends. Then, unexpectedly, a person whom you considered a good friend said something, or did something nasty to you. What happened? You probably spent the rest of the day thinking about it, worrying about it, getting mad about it. Your whole mood changed. From feeling elated, you began to feel deflated. What was happening? You began to live by the nasty word. That is the power of the human word. It can build up or it can pull down; it can elate or deflate; it can encourage or discourage.

Notice the power of a word. A word can actually change the

way you feel about yourself. There is an extraordinary irony here. If someone tried to push you out of the way, you would instinctively try to resist him or her. You would physically defend yourself. But if someone speaks a nasty word to you, the chances are that you will allow it to land on your heart.

I like to use the image of "landing rights" to illustrate the point I am trying to make. Before President George W. Bush could send his warplanes to the various "coalition countries" in preparation for the invasion of Iraq in 2003, the various countries involved had to give him "landing rights." It can be quite dangerous to give "landing rights" to warplanes. The country that does that becomes identified with the mission of the warplane. It is complicity in an act of war.

On the personal level, we can give "landing rights" to our hearts for anyone who wishes to engage in a war of words with us. We can allow every negative and destructive word to enter into our personal airspace, land unimpeded on our hearts, and change the way we feel about ourselves. We can become complicit in an act of war against ourselves and our own self-esteem.

The Power of Words

Why do words have such power in our lives? The reason is that on the deep, personal level, our spiritual level, we yearn for meaning and we live by the word that conveys meaning to us. We form our self-image through that meaning. The self-image controls the way we *feel* about ourselves. We are not born with a self-image: it is formed by the word that is spoken to us.

Sometimes the words spoken to us are constructive. They are supportive and kind, even when these words suggest some change in our behavior or views. Constructive words affirm and encourage, even when they seek to guide and correct. Perhaps the archetype of such constructive words is the relationship between a loving parent and child. The parent may chide and direct as well as praise, but in either case, the words used reflect loving concern and not indifference or dislike.

But sometimes the words spoken to us are destructive. These are the words of rejection and condemnation: words whose aim is to undermine and damage. Destructive words, too, may take the form of either praise or criticism. Praise that is dishonest and manipulative can be destructive. Similarly, criticism that aims to reject and condemn rather than to guide or teach is always destructive.

Constructive words are words that embrace and enrich life: they support us in fulfilling our potential. Destructive words reject and impoverish life: they hold us back. Notice that constructive and destructive words do not create a difference *in the world*. Rather, they create a difference *in attitude* toward the world, that is, a difference in how the world is seen and valued. The world can look entirely different depending on one's perspective.

Each of us has a choice between living in what I call the "house of the destructive word" or living in the "house of the constructive word." Where we choose to live, in this respect, is a profoundly *spiritual* choice. It rests on our decision whether or not to embrace or reject. And where we choose to live is a two-way street: Our perception of the world affects what we say and how we treat and value others. It affects what we hear and how we treat and value ourselves.

Healing the Self-Image

Many of us live, at least part of the time, in the house of the destructive word, mistaking it for reality. It is so easy to see why the self-image is damaged by living in this destructive place. Our focus is on all that is negative in ourselves and others, and, inevitably, we reject and devalue ourselves.

Healing starts with moving: from the house of the destructive word to the house of the constructive word. This change of attitude changes the way we address the world and ourselves. It is a spiritual change.

How does one make such a move? It is not easy. Moving house is always difficult: first taking the decision to move, accepting the changes and upheaval that it causes, and dealing with the practicalities. We can be very resistant even to thinking about moving. And very often, we need help with the practicalities involved.

"Moving House"

The very real benefits of moving from the house of the destructive word to the house of the constructive word are self-evident: who would choose to live in life-denying negativity, when they could live in life-affirming joy? Once one has seen the contrast, the problem is not really whether to move, but how to do it.

So many self-help writers seem instinctively to feel that we need help in making this move. They advocate seeking that help from a Higher Power. But how could that work?

For me, the Christian message is an invitation to move from the darkness of the house of the destructive word into the light and joy of the house of the constructive word, which is the creative word of God. Christ's teaching is a recipe for how to make this move.

Christ's Invitation to Move House

Whatever state we are in, whatever mess we may have made of life, Jesus' message to us is that salvation is always there for us. All we have to do is to reach out and accept it. All we have to do is to accept the universe as benevolent, that is, as the creative construction of a loving God. Jesus is inviting us to come to the home of a loving father.

For some, Christ's invitation and his message will instantly strike a chord of truth. But for many, the belief that it calls for is an act of faith. Acts of faith are hard, as this story shows:

A man falls over a high cliff. As he falls, he manages to catch hold of a small shrub. In despair, he calls out, "Help! Help! Is there anyone up there?" A voice answers, "Yes. I'm here. I'm God." The man cries, "O God, God, please save me!" God says, "And do you believe that I can save you?" The shrub is beginning to come away. The man cries out, "O God, God, I believe you can do anything! Please save me!" And God says, "And will you do everything I ask you to do?" The man replies, "Yes, God, I will do ANYTHING you ask me to do." God says, "OK, let go of the shrub." After a deadly silence, the man shouts, "Help! Help! Is there anybody else up there?"

We can all relate to this story. We may want to change our lives, but we are too scared to experiment with the things that might save us.

Jesus invites us to make his word our home. Jesus' word is, *always*, the constructive and creative word. His message is, *always*, that each of us matters to God, the way a child matters to a loving parent. In fact, we are the children of God! God's approach to us is like that of a good parent. It is always based on love for us, concern for us, and encouragement for us. No matter what we have done—or failed to do—this love and care are still there for us. We still matter to God. God's word to us is never rejection, never denigration, and never destructive. What have we to lose by accepting this invitation? What might we lose by being too scared even to try it out?

Some place must be home for heart and mind. The homeless heart and mind would be even more distressing than the homeless body. The home Jesus invites us to enter is a place where we can feel at ease. We can be ourselves, because we know that we are fully accepted. We know who we are; we have an identity as the son or daughter of the house, and the son or daughter of God. This perception of ourselves is instantly empowering. Our fears fall away. We are free, free to learn the truth about ourselves.

Precious in the Eyes of God?

Accepting Jesus' invitation opens up a way to move from the house of the destructive word to the house of the constructive word. We can reconstruct ourselves as the children of God, as precious to a higher power that we call God.

But accepting this kind of invitation, believing that we are precious to anyone, let alone to God, can be hard. Bad things happen in the world. We ourselves do bad things. We sometimes fail in the goals we have set for ourselves, and we fail to live up to the standards we hope for. What if, for some reason, we feel that we have forfeited any right to be loved? That we are no longer precious at all, but worthless or even repulsive?

It can be very difficult to accept that we are precious, that we matter to anyone, let alone God. I would like to share with you two examples of people for whom simply opening their hearts to this idea had a wonderful effect on their lives and happiness.

The first of these was a young priest, who came to Hawkstone Hall, the Redemptorist International Pastoral and Renewal Centre for priests, religious, and laity in Shropshire, England. He was concerned that he could not pray in the way he felt he should. He was a dynamic young man, who had taken over a parish from an old-fashioned priest who had been there for thirty-five years. The young priest modernized the parish. The people were delighted; they sang his praises. But this made him feel terrible. Because he felt he was not praying properly, their praises made him feel like a hypocrite. I asked him to read aloud from chapter fifty-three of the Book of Isaiah. When he came to the words "because you are precious in my eyes" (that is, in the eyes of God), I asked him to comment. He said, with great vehemence, "He is not referring to me." That was his problem: he felt that God had a high opinion of everyone else, but entertained a very low opinion of him. So, he lived in self-rejection. He had come to this conclusion because he thought he was failing: not holy enough, not prayerful enough, not zealous enough. But who imposed those tests of his worthiness on him? Not God: he did it himself. He had forgotten that we are all, including himself, precious in God's sight. There is no entrance test to God's love.

I asked him to accept Jesus' invitation to truly believe that, despite how he was judging himself, he remained God's precious child. This act of faith was made by embracing that liberating idea through a simple prayer of thanks to Jesus for this wonderful love. Within a few days, this truth had entered his heart and changed the way he saw and felt about himself, setting him free to live, pray, and grow again. The act of praying had set him free.

The second example is a woman who broke down in a panic when she was asked to be the first to introduce herself to a new group. We all felt for her. Later, I asked her about her reaction, and she told me that at about the age of twelve, a teacher had asked her to stand before the whole class and solve an arithmetic problem. She did not know how to do it. He humiliated her by calling her stupid and by having another student complete the problem instead. The teacher's cruel remark had robbed her of all her self-confidence, so that, years later, she was still seized by panic when asked to speak before a group—despite the fact that she had become a highly qualified nurse, working with people every day.

We asked this woman to put her trust in God, to truly believe that God could set her free from the destructive power of the word *stupid* that had so long been lodged in her heart. Together, through a simple prayer, we asked God to do this, and to fill her whole being with the conviction that she was precious in his sight. Before long, she was not only reading in public, but she composed a wonderful poem and recited it to the whole group. She was now living in the constructive house of God, a house of confidence and joy.

This young priest and this anxious woman had the courage to trust God. The practice of praying as if with confidence, a confidence that they may not have really felt at first, helped them to move from the house of the destructive word to the house of the constructive word.

The whole Bible is a long love letter from God, calling us all to trust him in this way. He wants us to live without fear, confident of his love, of the fact that we matter to him. He reassures us all:

> Do not fear, for I have redeemed you;
> I have called you by name, you are mine....
> Because you are precious in my sight,
> and honored, and I love you....
> Do not fear, for I am with you (Isaiah 43:1–5).

Christ's message is that, *whatever* we may have done or failed to do, we are still the beloved children of God and we still matter to God. The house of God's constructive, creative word, with all its power and healing, is still our home: Christ has given us the key to the door, and we need never be excluded again. All we have to do is to accept that gift.

Anything Goes, Then, in Christianity?

We tend to think that God has laws, and that if we break them, we forfeit his love and lose our place in his house. But, as Agnes Stanford, the great twentieth-century pioneer of the healing ministry used to say, "We cannot break God's law. If a man steps off the top of a precipice, he does not break the law of gravity, he just demonstrate it." In the same way, if we collide with divine law, that collision will not break God's law, it will break us.

Like any other good parent, God encourages his children in ways of living that are good for us, and discourages us from ways that are harmful and destructive. "Anything goes" is not a recipe for good parenting, whether human or divine. What good parent would condone a child abusing drugs or damaging their health in other ways? What good parent would condone a child's dishonesty, or physical violence, or antisocial behavior of other kinds?

Being precious in God's sight is not a license to behave however we like. Rather, it is a promise that, however we behave, we will still matter; we will still be relevant and important to God. We cannot cease to matter to God, and should not cease to matter to ourselves. We are always acceptable to God and should always be acceptable to ourselves.

Bad behavior, behavior that we *know* is wrong, wounds us very directly. How can one feel good about oneself, respect oneself, while behaving in ways one sees as bad? How can we live the truth that we are precious in God's sight, *good*, and behave in ways that are wholesome? Living the truth that we are all precious, no matter what, creates the motive to behave as such. It creates the motive to live well, behave well: to treat ourselves and others with the respect and dignity that come from being precious, from being the loved children of God.

Forgiveness

God does not condone bad behavior. But God forgives us, endlessly, and calls us to a better life. Forgiveness, too, is a way to move from the house of the destructive word to the house of the constructive word, as we shall see in more detail in chapter six.

Christ calls us to forgive endlessly, to "love our enemies" and do good to those who harm us. When we forgive those who hurt us—that is, forgive from the heart—we are exercising the mighty power of God's word. By living God's word as such, the broken heart is healed. We are living as the children of God.

We see the power of forgiveness in the life of Nelson Mandela. From the day he was released from prison—after being locked up for nearly thirty years, unjustly charged as a violent communist and dangerous revolutionary—has been preaching the truly revolutionary message of reconciliation. Remarkably, after such torment, he called on his own people, the oppressed and long-suffering black majority of South Africa, to forgive their white oppressors. Mandela sees clearly that it is not only the oppressed who need liberation; the oppressor is also in need of liberation. Reconciliation is the only road that leads to liberation. In his autobiography, he tells us how he fought the spiritual battle to survive as a freedom fighter in prison:

> Prison is designed to break one's spirit and destroy one's resolve. To do this the authorities attempt to exploit every weakness, demolish every initiative, negate all sign of individuality—all with the idea of stamping out that spark that makes each of us human and each of us who we are.[1]

That spark, which makes us human, is the image of God within us. Mandela understood clearly that if the prison authorities could make him hate, they would have broken his spirit. He was a prisoner for justice, not for revenge. He tells us about his experience when he stood as a prisoner in the court room where he had, as a lawyer, defended many people:

During the proceedings, the magistrate was diffident and uneasy, and would not look at me directly. The other attorneys also seemed embarrassed, and at that moment I had something of a revelation. These men were not only uncomfortable because I was a colleague brought low, but because I was an ordinary man being punished for his beliefs. In a way I had never quite comprehended before, I realized the role I could play in court and the possibilities before me as a defendant. I was a symbol of justice in the court of the oppressor, the representative of the great ideals of freedom, fairness and democracy in a society that dishonored those virtues. I realized then and there that I could carry on the fight even within the fortress of the enemy.[2]

By keeping his spirit free from bitterness and unforgiveness, Mandela did just that. As a prisoner for nearly thirty years, he inspired the struggle for freedom and justice in South Africa. He remained a free man in prison—free from hatred, from bitterness, from the desire for revenge. He became the first black president of South Africa and arguably the most influential statesperson of the last half of the twentieth century.

We must extend to ourselves the same forgiveness that we receive from God. I have often heard people declare, "I will never forgive myself for what I did." Isn't that a terrible thing to say to oneself? Unwillingness to forgive oneself may be a sign of a deep root of self-rejection. Such self-rejection imprisons us, cutting us off from the possibility of new growth and development.

After I spoke on this subject during a retreat at a maxium-security prison, one man came up to me and said, "I worshiped the ground my wife walked on, but I killed her. I can never forgive myself. I am getting out in a month's time. How can I forgive myself?" That man's inner world was shattered. Even though he was deeply repentant, he was still living in the house of the destructive word. How could he, a wife-killer, be precious in God's sight? After what he had done, how could he ever say, "I thank you for the wonder of myself"?

Among his fellow prisoners, there was a man who had been wrongly convicted of a terrible crime. This man, whose sentence has since been overturned by the Court of Appeal, had learned the secret of accepting himself, even in his dreadful situation. He was full of the Spirit of God, free from all bitterness at his unjust sentence. He took that murderer, ministered to him, and brought him into deep peace. He described his experience of the last night of the retreat in this way:

> How can I express in words the experience of Sunday evening? We gathered and prayed for the gift of the Holy Spirit in words and singing continuously. It was an experience of great joy. We prayed collectively for the gift of the Spirit for ourselves. Then we went individually to be prayed with. There was a continuous stream of people going up. Everyone was joyfully singing or praying. I could see great joy on the faces of everyone. It was out of this world.

As those prisoners, many of them deeply impressed by bad and bitter memories, opened their hearts to the Lord and forgave themselves with the same forgiveness they received from the Lord, there was "great joy on the faces of everyone." Even the grim circumstances of prison cannot rob people of the joy of the Lord.

The prisoners discovered the liberating power of forgiveness. First, we turned to the Lord for the forgiveness that we all need. Then, I invited them to forgive everyone who had ever hurt them, to share with them the forgiveness they had received. And, finally, I asked them to forgive themselves. I asked them to say this prayer: "Lord, I thank you for forgiving me my many sins. Now, Lord, I forgive myself. I thank you for the wonder of myself. I thank you that I am precious in your sight."

Forgiveness must never be confused with condoning or excusing. C. S. Lewis wrote:

> There is all the difference in the world between forgiving and excusing. Forgiveness says, "Yes, you have done this thing, but I accept your apology, I will never hold it against you and everything between us two will be exactly the same as it was before." But excusing says, "I see that you couldn't help it, or didn't mean it, you weren't really to blame." If one was not to blame then there is nothing to forgive. In this sense, forgiveness and excusing are almost opposite.[3]

Forgiveness sets us free to feel that we are precious, that we are valued. In accepting that there is something that needs to be forgiven, we are recognizing things that are destructive to us and to others. Through forgiveness, we recognize actions that come from the house of the destructive word and deed. And in that recognition, we are rejecting the house of the destructive and embracing the constructive. We are setting our feet on the path toward the constructive world, committing ourselves to it—yet another realization that we are special, that we are precious.

Embracing All That Is in Our Lives

However strongly one can accept oneself as precious, however powerfully one lives the constructive life, forgiving self and others, one may still have a problem from the past.

Sad memories from the past, hidden resentments, even bitterness can be the source of great pain and discouragement. These memories can haunt us, shaping or even distorting how we respond to the world long after the events themselves are past. How can we live in the house of the constructive word, with all of this painful baggage? How can we relate constructively to our past?

One thing is clear: denial, pretending that sad or bad events did not happen, will not do. In the first place, however much we refuse to think about them, it is hard to completely wipe negative events from our minds. They hide in our subconscious, ever ready to pop out and undermine us. In the second place, these bad experiences shaped who we are every bit as much as the positive experiences that we delight to remember. If we deny that, we cannot truly know who we are or what we are like. We would have a lopsided picture of ourselves.

For example, I know that I am the person I am today because of my lived experience: my early years as I grew in my family, leading into my primary and secondary education, my formation as a priest and a Redemptorist, and then the forty years that I have spent in priestly ministry. But that is only half the story. I am the person I am today through experiences of other kinds, too: my own sinfulness, the discouragement that I experienced from time to time, my failure at times to push myself to grow and develop, and the hurts and disappointments and frustrations that are part of life in a fallen world.

You may have been surprised, at one time or another, to hear someone who has suffered what seems to be an appalling disaster or tragedy say that it was the best thing that ever happened to them. The psychiatrist Irvin Yalom, for example, describes the case of a man dying of a painful cancer, whose psychological hang-ups had driven everyone (even other therapists) away from him in revulsion.[4] At first bitter and resentful, through therapy this man came to terms with his illness, his past, and his future. He became a different person, regaining the affection of others. As he was dying, he wrote what Yalom describes as the most moving thank you he had had from a client: "Thank you for saving my life." By embracing all that had happened in his life, and all that was to happen, this man had found a new peace and joy—just in time. He had moved from the house of the destructive word to the house of the constructive word. He recognized that without his disease, without his imminent death, this would never have happened.

Surprisingly, often when we look back on bad memories we can see that the events they reflect actually had unexpected effects on our lives. A lost job may seem like a disaster, but may push one into learning new skills, or to a change of direction, or a better life. Even our greatest failures or misfortunes may have pushed us to learn and develop.

So many people go through life filled with resentments about the past. The word *resent* comes from the Latin word *resentire*, which means "to feel again." When we nourish a resentful memory, we "feel again" the hurt from the past. It will remain a wound within until it is healed. Time does not heal inner wounds. The only way to have that wound healed is to live by the constructive word, the creative word of God.

If I find that I am filled with resentments or bitterness as I recall certain events, I know I am living by the destructive word: I am wounded, imprisoned in the house of the destructive word and living a life of low self-esteem. It is when I put those events in a proper perspective, letting go of the trauma of the past, that I am living in the house of the constructive word, set free to grow and develop.

The Secret of Inner Peace

Remember the centering prayer at the end of the last chapter. Exercises like this can bring an oasis of calm to our lives, a space in which we can begin to know ourselves, begin to approach spiritual questions.

In this second chapter, we have begun to look at another step along the journey toward spiritual development. This step moves beyond bodily stillness, and toward a peace of the spirit: a peace that comes from living in a constructive, affirming way, rejecting the negative and destructive. It moves toward that peace that comes from accepting ourselves as valuable, lovable, whatever may have happened to us, whatever we may have done, or not done.

Christ offers us a recipe for making this second move toward peace. He invites us to accept ourselves as the infinitely precious children of God. He invites us to feel the security of being loved, as a child feels secure in a loving home. He encourages us to be forgiving, to let go of resentments, and to embrace the positive.

Exercise

Center yourself, using the techniques we learned in the last chapter.

- Bring yourself to bodily stillness and calm.
- Now try to place yourself truly in the presence of your Higher Power, or God, enfolded in his love. How does that feel?
- Allow yourself to experience this feeling as powerfully as you can.
- Now focus again on your breathing.
- And bring yourself gently back to the world.

This technique, too, is a very old Christian form of prayer. With perseverance and patience, practicing this form of prayer can lead you to a profound sense of peace: a feeling that you are lovable, just as you are, however that may be.

3

Who Am I?

We are not human beings having a spiritual experience,
we are spiritual beings having a human experience.

PIERRE TEILHARD DE CHARDIN

Who is the self who is precious in God's eyes? Who is it, who is to be accepted, forgiven, embraced in entirety, loved *whole*, just as I am?

So much has been written about the self, from so many different perspectives. Surprisingly, there is no one universally agreed definition of what the self actually is. Think of all the different ways we use the word *self*: myself, themselves, ourselves, yourself; selfish, selfless; self-control, self-opinionated; not myself, beside myself, "I said to myself," and so forth.

Intuitively, we feel that when we use words like *me* and *I*, we refer to that which is deepest within us. But what is this? What forms and shapes it?

A Psychological View of Self

*Our understanding of our self starts
when we catch a glimpse
of ourselves in someone else's eyes.*[1]

We are not born with a self-image or a sense of self. In fact, the evidence is that at birth babies have so little sense of *self* that they do not recognize themselves as distinct and separate from the physical world around them at all. Understanding that objects exist independently of one's attention and act without regard to one's will takes time. Understanding that one is *a person*, understanding *who one is*, takes longer.

The Birth of "Self"

The discovery that we are separate and distinct from the physical universe and from other people is a major achievement, a milestone in early infancy. Exactly when babies begin to suspect the challenge of their separate existence is not clear. But by about nine months of age, they have started to get the basic idea. Gravity, and other laws of physics and nature, will operate, whether we like it or not. Other people will do pretty much as they wish, whatever we may want. Toward the end of their first year of life, babies grasp this in principle. But even in midlife or even in old age, we are still, often, coming to terms with this annoying, sometimes horrifying idea.

The discovery that we are unique and limited entities in this physical universe, separate from and unable to command and control events or experience, is the inevitable consequence of interacting with the world. Nature has its own rules and is a stern teacher. Our inability to fly unaided, or to walk through walls, our separation within one organic and fragile body from the rest of creation—these are nonnegotiable aspects of existence. We can discover them for ourselves. But we do not need much understanding of these things in order to know our "self." In reality, none of us can fly, or walk through walls. Such things do not differentiate us as individuals, and our concept of "self" is fundamentally about our human individuality.

What makes me an individual, different and distinct from all the other individuals around me? In answering this question, we begin to define ourselves in relation to others. For example: *Who am I?* "I am Jane's husband, John's father, the headmaster of the village school." These roles define *who I am* in my social context, the roles I play in relation to others. "I am tall, clever, and witty"—even these apparently individual characteristics are defined in relation to others. To see myself as tall, for example, I must notice that others around me are generally shorter. To see myself as clever, I must compare myself to the norm.

Charles H. Cooley, a pioneer of psychological research in this area, described our understanding of "self" as a "looking glass" self.[2] That is, who I am is so tightly bound up with how I relate to other people that I try to understand who I am and how worthy I am by trying to understand how others see me. I cannot be a headmaster, if no one else accepts me in that role; nor clever, if everyone around me believes me stupid. Our understanding of our "self" begins, then, when we see ourselves through other people's eyes.

Of course, we cannot truly know how others see us. We cannot read their minds, and we may misinterpret their behavior or their words. Our understanding of how others see us is always based on our own inferences and theories. It's a construction, not an objective view. We extrapolate and imagine how others would see us or how others would judge us, if they only knew everything about us. Whether they know or not, we feel the emotions appropriate to how we imagine they would respond.

We feel pride if we are judged well, and shame if we are criticized.

This sense of "self" embraces all that we think we are: our physical and psychological attributes, the roles we play, our strengths and weaknesses.[3] And it has two major components: our description of our self, which forms our *identity*, and our evaluation or judgment of that identity, which is our *self-esteem*.[4] Both are projected to us through other people's eyes.

Why Do Others Matter So Much to Us?

Why do we let other people's judgments play such a large part in our understanding of ourselves and our feelings about ourselves? The answer lies at the heart of human nature: we are a profoundly *social* species. We *must* live with others, interact with them, give and receive support and love, for our health, if not our very survival. All human existence is coexistence. This means that we are very powerfully motivated to get along with other people, to have their affection and approval. By looking at how others see us, we can gauge how well we are integrated into our community and how much we are valued. If we do not fit well enough or are not well thought of, we are able to utilize such feedback to adjust our behavior.

Each of us has a profound need to *matter* to other people.[5] That is to say, we need to believe that we are relevant to someone, that others care about what we do and whether we live or die. We need someone who values us and respects us. We need to be needed. The feeling of mattering to other people is an extremely powerful thing.[6] People will go to extraordinary lengths and suffer extraordinary pains and privations for those to whom they matter, and who matter to them. One has only to think of the sacrifices made by parents for their children, or by soldiers for their comrades, or by nurses for their patients, to see the power of mattering. The very strong "mattering" we feel when we fall in love, or have a child, is an immensely joyful, life-giving thing. As a celibate priest I know the life-giving joy of being able to commit my life, my talents, and my time to helping people find meaning in life, solace in grief, peace in trouble, and forgiveness and reconciliation in their hearts when they feel alienated or unworthy. I know my father and mother had the same life-giving joy as they committed their lives to each other and to bringing up their family. They knew they mattered to their children, just as I know I matter to those I help.

Conversely, there are few feelings more devastating and desolating than the feeling that one does not matter to a living soul. The need to matter gives us a powerful incentive to take other people's opinions of us seriously. We internalize their opinions, accepting them as accounts of our *self*. We judge ourselves as others would. This is normal. It can, however, be either encouraging or very disheartening. There is nothing sadder, for instance, than to hear a person say, "I don't matter." A person is at great risk who believes that what they say or do makes no difference because they matter to no one. We cannot live without meaning. Without a purpose for life, without mattering to someone, a person may well opt out of life, and end it tragically.

Taking Possession of Ourselves

From a psychological point of view, then, our understanding of ourselves is very much rooted in how other people view us. Does this mean that there is no core "me," no "me" that stands separate from how others see me? Does my view of myself, my feeling about myself, my individuality, come entirely from "outside"?

We human beings are reflective creatures. That is to say, we think and reflect on everything we do. For example, we not only see a pattern or a shape in the clouds, we are also attentive to such abstract reflection. We consciously reflect on our interpretation of the cloud. Why do I interpret the pattern in *that* particular way? Why do I not see it as something else? We not only act and think, we also watch ourselves doing those things, and we build up theories about our own minds and about ourselves.

One obvious fruit of such reflection is the observation that each and every one of us plays many different roles in life. An individual may be, for example, at one and the same time, an accountant, a Sunday schoolteacher, a father, a son, a brother, a husband, an amateur actor, a gardener, and so on. In each of these roles, the individual has an identity: a set of attributes that are brought into play in that situation, and a set of skills, or strengths and weaknesses, that may be unique to that one role. There may be a very great difference between the identity a man has in his role as father, and that which he has in the cut and thrust of his work, or the tranquillity of his garden, or among friends in the pub. In fact, this same individual may behave and perceive himself (and be perceived by others) in very different ways across different roles or situations. And each identity has its own level of self-esteem: a man may feel very good about his role as an accountant, for example, while despairing of his failures as a husband.

Recognizing that our identity and our self-esteem are fragmented across different roles in this way poses a problem. The feeling that one is fragmented, that there is no consistency at one's core, that there is no integrated "self" in there, is a very noxious one. It can feel very much like psychological disintegration: *I don't know who I am.* We are highly motivated to avoid that sort of feeling. In fact, psychological health rests very much in the sensation of having a consistent identity, being the same self at heart, across situations and roles.

We use our powers of reflection to work toward a consistent, integrated understanding of who we are, making judgments that give us a degree of control over our sense of self, rather than leaving us the passive recipients of other people's views. For example, some of the identities we bear are more important than others, and some are more relevant than others, as this example shows:

> Since my adult son went away to the university, I have become, perforce, a domestic tidier—not a role in which I have ever excelled. But being a domestic tidier is a role thrust upon me, and one that I do not value much or view as important—almost certainly because I am no good at it. And at least while I am the only one at home and there is no one to criticize things, it is also a role of low relevance. Recognizing my low worth in that particular role does not normally damage my sense of my overall identity or self-esteem, which is based on other roles that are more important or more relevant to me. But let my mother-in-law come for a visit, and the relevance and importance of cleaning the kitchen as opposed to writing a research report will be dramatically reversed—with bad effects on my self-esteem. But even now, my powers of reflection can protect my self-image; I downplay the "badness" of being untidy by prominently displaying a fridge magnet that supports my values with the legend: "Dull women have immaculate houses."

Thus we pick and choose between the various identities that make up our overall sense of self and self-esteem, and we shape our self-judgments to reflect the identities that are important or relevant to us. By editing our self-image in this way, we have begun to take personal responsibility for our sense of self, rather than simply letting ourselves be described and judged by others. Through this kind of editing process we can find a consistent identity, a consistent sense of who we are, and what it is that gives us the individuality that transcends different situations and roles. And through such reflective editing, we can choose to protect good self-esteem by valuing what we are good at and devaluing what we are bad at, as the example quoted above shows. Conversely—or perhaps perversely—we can elect to devalue ourselves by focusing on what we are not good at.

This search for consistency does not, of course, mean that we have a simple, straightforward view of ourselves. In fact, we may experience ourselves as complex, many-layered beings full of contrasts and even conflicts. This is captured very well by the reflections of a great Russian spiritual leader, Baroness de Hueck Doherty. She was a spiritual writer and founder of the Madonna House Apostolate (a contemplative lay community based in Canada). When she was already over eighty she gave an interview in which she talked about the "selves" she knew on her spiritual journey. She said:

It's like there are three persons inside me. There's someone I call "the Baroness." The Baroness is spiritual and given to asceticism and prayer. She is the religious person. She's the one who founded the religious community, wrote the spiritual books and who tries to give her life to the poor. It's the Baroness who's impatient with the things of this world and who tries to keep her eyes focused on the things beyond this life.

But inside me too there is another person whom I call Catherine. Catherine is first of all and always a woman who enjoys fine things, luxuries, sensual delight. She likes idleness, long baths, fine clothes, putting on makeup, good meals, good wine, and used, as a married woman, to enjoy a healthy sex life. Catherine enjoys this life and doesn't want renunciation or poverty. She's not religious like the

Baroness. Indeed, she hates the Baroness and has a strained relationship with her.

And finally, inside me too, there's someone else, a little girl lying on a hillside in Finland, watching the clouds and daydreaming. The little girl is different still from both the Baroness and Catherine.

And as I get older, I feel more like the Baroness, long more for Catherine, but think that maybe the little girl daydreaming on the hillside in Finland might be who I really am.[7]

Of course, the Baroness is not talking about the "split personality" or alter egos of Hollywood dramas. These are not alternative personas seizing control at different times; rather they are different facets of one complex human being, who happens to be able to articulate and accept that complexity rather more clearly than most of us—who are just as complex—are able to do.

Self As a Work in Progress

One thing that emerges very clearly from this psychological account is that our sense of self must, inevitably, grow and change through life. Our sense of self is always a work in progress.[8]

The social roles we play change in systematic ways as we grow up, pass through adult life, and grow older. A baby at birth may, for example, be a son and a grandson. By early childhood, he is also a brother, a schoolboy, the best football player on the street, and a member of a church. By adolescence, he has become perhaps a boyfriend, the local paperboy, and a university candidate. In adult life, some of these accumulated roles will continue and some will drop away (being a child or a schoolboy, for instance), and new roles will be added such as being a husband, an accountant, a father, a golfer, and so on.

As roles change through life, we acquire new identities and new people who matter, new people whose judgments matter. The relevance and importance of certain roles will change through life. For example, being a son or daughter may be the crucial role for a child, but a minor one for a person of fifty. Conversely, being a doctor is a game to a five-year-old, but the key identity for someone at forty. Important roles may be lost through disaster or through the inevitable effects of aging, such as widowhood, divorce, retirement, or redundancy. Perceptions of our efficacy and worth in any role may change as we or other people change, or as we acquire or lose competency, or as we succeed or fail to maintain a heavy workload, and so on.

Our understanding of ourselves grows and changes through these patterns of shifting roles, relevancies, and levels of importance throughout life, from birth to death. And it is not just the character of the roles that we play that changes as we pass through life: the younger the child, the fewer roles he or she plays, and the fewer people there are in his or her life who matter and whose judgments matter. With less varied experiences to pick and choose between, the younger the child the more vulnerable the self-image is to success or failure in any one role, or to criticism or praise from any one individual. As we become adult, our horizons expand, we take on more and more roles, and have more scope for choosing what will or will not matter to us, what will or will not define our sense of who we are and how we feel about ourselves. This broader range of experience gives adults a greater robustness to other people's opinions than is possible in childhood. In later life, the range of roles played and the number of people who matter may both dwindle. Although this inevitably affects the self-image, it does not create a vulnerability as profound as the young child's, because in later life we still have a vast range of past experience to call on, and far greater mental resources than the young child.

It is not just the roles that we play that change through life. Our ability to reflect, and so to take possession of our own identity, grows and changes through life, reflecting growth and change in our knowledge and understanding, and in the power of our reasoning.

The very young baby has more or less no capacity for reflection on the self. At birth, he or she is profoundly unaware even of there being a "self" to reflect on, as we have already seen. Becoming aware of a sense of self is not a one-step process from unawareness to awareness. Rather, the capacity to reflect on oneself develops gradually right through childhood, and on through adult life, as we become more knowledgeable and more able to think and reason.

Understanding is, at first, fragmented. The young child does not have enough breadth of knowledge to draw analogies between one situation and another, or to draw out abstract principles, and so to see connections or patterns across situations. Reflections of young children are generally very concrete and very specific.

For example, a young child may not have enough knowledge of human behavior or motives to understand concepts such as "mean" or "generous." The child may know that Jane is nice because she gave him a toy, and that Mary is horrid because she stole his biscuit. But these opinions reflect the very specific circumstances in which they arise: the giving of the toy, the stealing of the biscuit. They are not interpreted in terms of any general trait that Mary or Jane may have, such as being mean or generous. Because the child does not yet understand these general traits, he cannot use them to predict how Mary or Jane might behave in other situations—as an adult might. Thus the young child may know that no one likes Robert and everyone likes Jack, but have no real understanding of what it is about Robert or Jack that this reflects.

The younger the child, the less he or she understands about human behavior, thought, feeling, or motivation. Consequently, the younger the child, the less able he or she is to see patterns in an individual's behavior, to identify these as a trait, and to make predictions or interpretations in the light of these patterns. This greatly limits children's ability to interpret or form opinions about other people. Equally importantly, it limits their ability to see patterns in themselves, and so to find a consistent basis for their sense of self or their self-image. Their identity is fragmented by comparison with an adult's and provides no strong basis for tempering the judgments others make of them.

Unable to put other people's judgments of them in a broader context, young children literally have no resources to refute a bad judgment, or to notice that although they are judged to be naughty *just now*, this is not characteristic of them and need not be part of their identity. They simply accept what others say about them, uncritically. They allow others to define who they are and how they are.

Both the limited roles the child plays and the limited ability to reflect contribute to the vulnerability of the young child's self-image and self-esteem. Once we put ourselves in the child's position, it's easy to see why factors that affect self-esteem in childhood have a special potency that can leave a lasting legacy. The idea that I am *bad* or *stupid* may lodge deeply in the child's mind, unexamined, accepted as an absolute fact, difficult to bring out and examine in later life. Even an adult person may live by those childhood descriptions of himself or herself. Some people may never shake themselves free from the aspersions cast on them as children. They never begin the mature process of taking responsibility for their own identity, for defining themselves for themselves and living up to their own definition. They continue to allow others to define them and then embark on the fruitless journey of living up to other people's definitions.

As we grow older, our ability to understand human behavior and motivations grows. We become adept at identifying patterns or traits in others and in ourselves, and in editing our descriptions to pick out the consistent themes that define our individuality, or that of someone else. We become adept at putting a particular comment in context—*he put me down because he is jealous,* for example—allowing us to discount the putdown. We decide which roles matter to us, whose opinions matter, and edit and construct our view of ourselves accordingly. Through this process, we progressively take charge of who we are; we take possession of, and responsibility for, ourselves, rather than being at the mercy of other people's opinions.

Very importantly, this taking possession of ourselves involves identifying our values: what is it that I respect or enjoy? What is it that I admire or aspire to? As I explore these things, I gradually construct a model of my "ideal self," the person I would like to be, the person I feel I am meant to be: the "real me." Progressively, this "ideal self" becomes the benchmark for my judgment of myself. It becomes my inner critic, my basis for self-acceptance or self-rejection, for pride or shame. And in so doing, it begins to shape my development, as I try to make my behavior consistent with that ideal self. Development becomes a voyage toward the ideal self I have constructed.

Values change as we grow older, reflecting increases in our understanding of the world and the developmental progress we have made. We come to a better understanding of what it means, for example, to be a good teacher, or a good parent, and we value and encourage those traits in ourselves, judge ourselves in terms of their presence or absence. And we grow beyond particular social roles (teacher, parent, and so on), both as we take on more roles, and as we age and start to drop them. Our search for consistency in the self through all of this change pushes us progressively to search for values that transcend particular situations or roles: values that will apply across many different situations; values that can serve us when the particular roles we have played in life are over. We move beyond values rooted in roles, toward values more rooted in inner conviction. In the process, our search for consistency in our experience of self inevitably pulls us toward values that are abstract and general. Such values are often moral or spiritual values, for these are the values that provide the most universal basis for regulating our interactions with others, and for our ultimate evaluations of ourselves. So, we begin to talk about justice, truth, integrity, and authenticity. I may still want to be a good teacher or a good golfer, but I know that it is more important to be a good person. And the skills needed to be a good person will make me a better teacher (and maybe even a better golfer).

The Healthy Self

In a healthy individual, the sense of self is rooted in reality. That is to say, the identity we understand ourselves to bear matches up, more or less, to the collective view of who and what we are with respect to feedback from the world. We have a more or less accurate perception of our attributes, strengths, and weaknesses. There is little self-delusion. Truthful self-knowledge allows us to set realistic targets for ourselves. A young woman will not set her heart on being a brain surgeon, for example, if she knows she lacks the academic ability to enter medical school. Honest, healthy self-knowledge guides our ambitions and choices toward achievable goals and identities. By setting such realistic targets, we have a good chance of meeting our aspirations and achieving good self-esteem.

Good self-esteem means that one respects and values oneself—as we all need to do—to be healthy. The feeling of regarding oneself as worthless is one of the most destructive and desolating of all human experiences. But to be healthy, our evaluation of ourselves must be balanced and based in accurate self-perception. If we tell ourselves we are wonderful, clever, and successful, but we have no achievements to back this up, and others see us as dull, foolish, and ordinary, we are setting ourselves up for a thousand attacks on our self-esteem each day. We must fight off threatening feedback from reality in order to maintain our inflated view of ourselves. Conversely, if we focus entirely on our failings, overlooking our strengths, we are equally out of touch with reality: we bring ourselves low where a more balanced view would paint a different picture.

Self-esteem is a fragile thing. Despite all our reflective powers, we are still vulnerable to outside influences. We may fail in some important task we have chosen, for example, despite our best efforts. Or we may be forced to work in a job to which we are not suited and with which we struggle, and so be forced to adopt values that we cannot live up to. Or we may be unable to escape the criticisms of someone we live with or work with, someone who has power or authority over us, and whose opinion we cannot ignore. Choosing which roles to focus on in forming our identity and self-esteem is not always enough to protect our self-image.

Nor can we always or immediately find consistent themes across different identities that matter to us. How does a gentle father, for example, integrate that identity with his reputation as an aggressive player at work?

Self-esteem, our very self-image, is not a constant thing. It can fluctuate with events, over minutes or years. It can change as our skills, insight, and values change—or as they fail to change and develop to meet our new circumstances or new roles in life. The construction and care of a healthy self, a healthy self-esteem, is a lifelong task.

49

A Spiritual View of Self

Our understanding of our self starts
when we catch a glimpse
of ourselves in someone else's eyes.

A psychological understanding of "self," of who we are, roots that understanding in our perception of ourselves through other people's eyes, and in our need to "belong," to matter to others. My Christian perspective would not argue with that view; as Pope John Paul II wrote, in his first encyclical, "a person cannot survive without love."[9]

We cannot get to know our real self in isolation. We have to be in communion, in friendship with others. I can know myself to the extent that I allow myself to be known by others. It is through their knowledge of me that I can come to a new knowledge of myself. As Paul Wadell writes:

> It is true that much of our sense of self is derived from our capacity to acknowledge the uniqueness of another inasmuch as their uniqueness becomes a reflection of our own, but that is only part of the picture. Some of our identity comes from how we are recognized by them. So much of who we are is a measure of the attention we have received; so much of how we think of ourselves, our appreciation of self, our self-image, and identity is other-bestowed. This reciprocity is exactly what makes friendship so morally important to securing identity. We gain some sense of self in recognizing another, but we gain more sense of self in being recognized, in being acknowledged and responded to in love. In large measure, how we recognize ourselves depends on how we have been recognized and appreciated by others.[10]

This is very much the "looking glass" self of which psychologists have written.

But a spiritual understanding of "self" cannot wholly be captured by the self that is defined in relation to other people. A scientific account places "self" in a universe defined by biological, psychological, and social processes. Is that all there is to us? Is that all we amount to? Instinctively, we feel that *it is not*. The influential psychologist and counselor Carl Rogers, at the end of his life, said that his one regret was that he had overlooked the spiritual nature of the human being. From a spiritual perspective, we are far more than the sum of biological, psychological, and social processes; we also have a transcendental nature, a self that takes part in the nature of God.

The True Self

Spirituality identifies a number of elements in the self. There is the self that is rooted in biological, psychological, and social processes, defining itself in terms of its possessions, its role-based identities, its relationships and skills and its public reputation in the here and now. This self is fragile, ephemeral, and transient. We must *live* it, play the roles assigned to it, respect and nurture it. We have no choice in that. But this self will pass away, changing as our material circumstances and roles change, or as other people's opinions of us change. It will end, as our bodies decay and die. This "outer" self is vulnerable: it can be damned by poor opinion from unkind minds. And it has hurdles to jump, standards to meet: it is locked in competition, always exposed to the possibility of failure. This transient self is not the measure of our being. Nevertheless, it is the vehicle for our transcendental nature.

This inner transcendental nature is the heart of our real value and meaning. Deep down, we feel that we are more than the roles we play, more than our possessions or positions in life; more than the pretenses we make to gain acceptance and approval. We transcend those things: we are spiritual creatures. And as spiritual creatures, precious in God's eyes, we are eternal and constant. We are known to God. That is, our basic essence is unique, precious, beloved, and anticipated by God from the beginning of time, and will remain forever. At this level, our understanding of ourselves starts, not from catching a glimpse of ourselves in other people's eyes, but from seeing our true selves through the eyes of God. And in those eyes, we are precious just as we are: there is no cruel rejection, no possibility of failure, death, or decay. There is only the danger of failing to find or failing to acknowledge that true self, failing to become the person we are meant to be.

Self As Our Capacity for God

Psychology focuses on the mechanics of human existence. How can a blob of matter, a bunch of atoms, come to think and feel? What processes transform a single cell, a fertilized egg into such a complex creature? Theology, by contrast, focuses less on *how* and more on *why*. Why do we exist at all? What is the point of it all? And where psychology simply assumes that we are just another complex biological entity, theology asks: *What, exactly, are we?*

Saint Irenaeus, one of the earliest of the great theologians, argued that our true self is not a "given," not a preexisting entity. Rather, it is something that develops through life. We do not automatically become our true selves. Rather, to fulfill our destinies, we must be endlessly open to receiving the Spirit of God. Through the gifts of the Holy Spirit—the Spirit of God—we become a complete and whole person, the person we truly are.

Thus I experience an inner urge or call to be fully human, to "be myself," a self that is genuine and sincere, a self that is honest and truthful, a self that is compassionate and considerate, a self that accepts responsibility for life with all its implications. This call to be fully human energizes true human development: that is, moral, spiritual, and physical development.

Through the ages men and women have reflected on this inner call, this interior urge to become the person they deep down believe that they are meant to be. People have always been conscious of an "inner voice," an interior guide that points the way. We have always called it *conscience*. We accept and respect the inviolability of conscience. The freedom of conscience is the most basic freedom each of us enjoys.

Each person has a conscience, an inner awareness of the difference between right and wrong. As we develop, we begin to accept that fidelity to conscience is the path to wholeness, health, and maturity. We experience that "going against our conscience" is an extraordinarily painful thing to do. It leaves a scar, or a mark, that we call guilt. We know instinctively that to describe people as "having no conscience" is about the worst possible thing we can say about them. We know that our dignity as persons, our authenticity, and our very integrity depend on our fidelity to our own conscience.

Where does this conscience come from? Is it a psychological or spiritual phenomenon, or both? We shall return to this question in chapter seven. Here it is worth saying that, for a Christian, conscience may involve the psychological, but it is also a part of our capacity for God and our oneness with God. Here is a passage from a Catholic document expressing this view:

Deep within his conscience man discovers a law which he has not laid upon himself but which he must obey. Its voice, ever calling him to love and to do what is good and to avoid evil, tells him inwardly at the right moment: do this, shun that. For man has in his heart a law inscribed by God. His dignity lies in observing this law, and by it he will be judged. His conscience is man's most secret core, and his sanctuary. There he is alone with God whose voice echoes in his depths. By conscience, in a wonderful way, the law is made known which is fulfilled in the love of God and of one's neighbor. Through loyalty to conscience Christians are joined to other men in the search for truth and for the right solution to so many moral problems which arise both in the life of individuals and from social relationships. Hence, the more a correct conscience prevails, the more do persons and groups turn aside from blind choice and try to be guided by the objective standards of moral conduct.[11]

The development of conscience becomes a voyage toward the ideal self we have constructed. Fidelity to conscience is the only way to arrive at our destination. We are made in the image of God! Reflecting on this, Heather Ward has described our experience of self as *our capacity for God.*[12] Our search for our true self is really a search for God. Self-fulfillment becomes a reality when we open our lives to God as we understand God, to the "higher power" in our life.

Finding the True Self

The material self, the self that is defined entirely by external criteria and judgments, looks constantly for recognition, affirmation, and reassurance from others. It is deeply embedded in the particular values of the specific roles it plays: the good teacher, the good parent. In a mad, bad society, its values will often be bad. Its horizons are limited and material. This material self looks always "outwards" for its endorsement of itself.

By contrast, the true self looks inward, toward its own values, valuing its unrepeatable, individual uniqueness. Its horizons are infinite and universal: it looks to the ultimate values of life, not to the immediate gratifications. It looks to the values that come from God.

How can we find this "true self"? We must rise above the material, the immediate. We must set our sights on God. But this "true self" will not come to us automatically. We must work for it. We do not construct it or invent it, because it is in the image of God, *given* for all time.

From this perspective, our human life becomes a voyage toward the self we are meant to be, the self we are in God's eyes: the "true" self. We cannot directly know the mind of God anymore than we can directly know the mind of another human being. We can only open our hearts and minds to God, draw inferences, and develop our understanding. We seek to understand what God calls us to be, what God wants us to be. And we strive to become our true self.

The Psychological and Spiritual: Two Worlds or One?

Psychological and spiritual views of the self are different at many levels. The first presents us very much in the context of the natural world, as biological creatures seeking an understanding of ourselves and our worth as a means of relating better to other members of our species, to our society. In this view, we are finite, transient creatures defined by our circumstances and psychological character. The second presents us in the context of God, as spiritual beings searching for an understanding of God and a better relationship with God. In this view, we are eternal, immortal beings, defined by our likeness to God. Psychological accounts very often simply ignore the possibility of a spiritual dimension to the self. Sometimes, unfortunately, spiritual accounts seem to reject the psychological self as almost a distraction or illusion: an outer shell that is not "real," not our real self at all.

Spiritual accounts should never reject the psychological self, though they will refuse to be confined or restricted to material processes. There is more to being human than meets the psychological eye. Spiritual accounts are concerned with this "more."

A New Synthesis

Is it possible to believe that human psychology is purely mechanical, or purely the product of biological processes, or that we no more transcend our physical lives than does a snail, say, or a robot? Surely, few of us experience ourselves like that. We yearn to transcend our mortal limitations. We yearn for a spiritual life that goes beyond the here and now. We feel, profoundly and instinctively, that we are more than the sum of the elements and processes that make us.

And is it possible to believe that we could be shaped as spiritual beings, yet also sent into this world armed with a mass of irrelevant or even destructive psychological processes that we must fight against in our search for God? Certainly, a loving God is more likely to have equipped us with useful tools than with distracting ones.

What if my outer psychological self is the starting point, the tool through which my journey toward my transcendental self is shaped and guided? What if my human and psychological nature is, in fact, designed for God? What if it is designed to lead me on my journey toward God?

At first, this idea seems strange, even absurd. How could such a limited thing as human psychology, resting as it does in neurological and biological mechanisms, in atoms of carbon and water, possibly be the instrument through which we take the measure of the infinity of God? How could our prosaic, pedestrian, psychological nature capture the glory of God? And yet...

On your wrist is an improbable collection of metal, plastic, leather. A very limited, mechanical thing, a thing defined and circumscribed by very finite factors. But what it measures is ephemeral, immense, perhaps eternal: it measures *time*, and makes that invisible dimension visible to us. A tool may be prosaic, and yet capture something that far transcends its prosaic nature. If a wristwatch can do it, why not human psychology?

This way of thinking puts human psychology and spirituality back together in a new way. My human self is not to be rejected or despised, but loved, as the instrument through which I may know God. The integration of the psychological and the spiritual gives us a new and richer picture of what it is to be human, and what it means to say that we have a true self that is our capacity for God. It allows us to ask afresh: *Who am I?*

I Am Someone Who Needs to Matter, Who Needs to Matter to God

I am someone who needs to matter to other people: to be relevant to them, to be valued by them, to be needed by them. This need to matter is at the core of what it is to be human. It is the essence of what holds us together in families, in friendships, in communities, and in societies. Not to matter to anyone! To be cut off from all human relationships! That would be a desolate experience indeed. That complete isolation would be a form of death: for how can I exist, in relation to *nothing*?

Vital as they are, human relationships are transient, fragile, ephemeral. Friendships, families, marriages come and go, as we change, lose contact, have misunderstandings and die. We yearn to matter to someone who is constant, eternal, and free of our human limitations. Only our relationship with God can be eternal. Only our relationship to God can be perfect. Understanding that we matter to God, and that God matters to us, provides the ultimate experience of mattering. *I am someone who needs to matter to God.*

I Am Someone Who Needs to Discover Myself Through Other Eyes

Our need to matter, our need to relate to others shows us the way out of isolation. We look at ourselves through other people's eyes, judging ourselves as we imagine they would judge us, and using those judgments to shape ourselves so that we may relate to them better. This is the first, most primitive psychological tool for discovering the self: we internalize other's views and judgments of us, we make them our own, and so get our first view of who we are. We are all, to a degree, "people pleasers."

But human views of us vary and change. Different people may have different views of us. Seeing ourselves purely through other human eyes would give only a fragmented, transient picture of our self. And that picture is earthbound!

We long to find a consistent understanding of self, of who we really are and of who it is that is essentially the same, across different situations, experiences, and years. Inevitably, this longing pushes us toward self-examination; toward a reflection on what we value and what we do not value, what is important or relevant to us and what is not. Through such reflections we begin to take possession of our self, begin to shape and direct it in the light of our core values. We build up an image of self, an image of our ideal self, an image that becomes our guide in directing our development. This core-self image seeks to embrace ever wider aspects of our experience. To achieve this, it must, progressively, discover more abstract and general values, values that will apply over wider and wider experience. Inevitably, these abstract values tend toward the moral and the spiritual, for moral and spiritual values are, above all, about our relationship to one another and to the universe. At the end of the day it is the *quality* of our relationship with the universe that really matters, whether we are loving, kind, caring, and compassionate, or whether we are a hardhearted millionaire. The quality of our relationship with the universe is a measure of our true value.

It is worth commenting that psychological processes do not invent the self or its values from out of the blue: these things are a reflection of something greater than the individual, whether that be the opinions of society at large, the natural laws governing human interactions or the spiritual nature of God. Our understanding of self is a process of discovery of these things that stand above and beyond us, and of our relationship to them.

Thus psychological processes, in their search for a consistent self that transcends the particular circumstances of the day, push us toward a search for the spiritual: a search for God. Psychological processes open the way for us to find our spiritual selves, and so to find God. They allow us to begin to view ourselves in relation to God, and to try to see ourselves through God's eyes. Psychological processes, in other words, provide the tools we need to answer the call of God, to open ourselves to receive his Spirit, and to grow toward him—that is, toward the self that is in the image of God.

A New Self

Our human understanding of self is always a work in progress, always changing, and always developing through life. Sometimes we may get bogged down, or "stuck," in a particular way of seeing ourselves: for example, we may get stuck with the prosaic values of everyday life, with the purely human and material world, and with other people's views of us. Sometimes it takes something dramatic to jog us out of a rut or to start us growing and developing again.

Even if psychological processes provide the tools for our journey toward God, the mere possession of these tools does not guarantee that we will use them efficiently and achieve those ends, or even that we will use them at all.

My faith tells me that God is there, willing us on, calling us to him. We must, therefore, be ready to open our hearts to his Spirit. Jesus speaks of a "new self," a self living in him and so in God, a self created not by us but by God. This self lives in awareness of God, and in the light of spiritual values that come from God. This is our true self, the self we are searching for, voyaging toward. This is the self we are called to be.

Accepting the True Self

The individual that I am in this human life may be good or bad, competent or incompetent. He or she may be praised and proud of achievements, or criticized and ashamed of mistakes or failures—fairly or otherwise. These things can seem vital. They can seem to be the only important thing in life.

A poor self-concept, a low self-esteem can dominate our perception of ourselves, and block our path to God: how could anyone, even God, see such a wretched failure, such a bad person as precious? We hide away from God in shame. *He cannot love the person I actually am.* But this way of thinking misses the point.

My faith tells me that I am far more than my present human life suggests. *I am a work in progress.* The self I am right now is a mere fraction of what I have been and what I will be. It is a mere fraction of what I *can* be; for I am a creature endowed with the capacity for discovering God, for discovering myself as the image of God. That astonishing capacity lifts me beyond the happenstance of this present moment. It places me in juxtaposition to the eternal. That capacity for God defines me, defines the nature of what I am, what I truly am. And it is this capacity that commands my reverence and respect. It is this capacity that makes me, always, precious in God's eyes.

Exercise

Center yourself, using the technique we learned at the end of chapter one.

- Bring yourself to stillness and calm.
- Let yourself feel enfolded absolutely in the love of your Higher Power, God, as we started to do in the exercise at the end of chapter two.
- In that loving place, that safe place, think about yourself, about all the roles that you play, your activities, your joys and hurts.
- Love yourself, just as you are right now. How does that feel?
- Love yourself as powerfully as you can.
- Now focus again on your breathing.
- And bring yourself gently back to the world.

This, too, is a very old Christian form of prayer. Jesus tells us to love our neighbors as we love ourselves (Mark 12:31). He is reminding us that we must love ourselves if we are to love others properly. Loving yourself and doing what is good for yourself is a form of prayer. It is looking after someone who is precious to God and who has the capacity to discover God. Like learning to still our bodies, and like learning to feel enfolded by the love of God, learning to love ourselves fully takes time and practice: it takes perseverance and patience.

4

Core Beliefs and Self-Esteem

*Crawling aboot like a snail in the mud
covered wi' clammy blae
Me, made after the image o' God—
Jings! But it's laughable, tae."*

JOE CORRIE, POET AND MINER, SCOTLAND

What are the values that shape our understanding of ourselves, of our identity? Where do these values come from? What effects do they have on our lives?

The values we embrace form the standard against which we judge ourselves. Our evaluation of how well we match up to that standard is the basis of our self-esteem. As the psychologist Stanley Coopersmith puts it:

By self-esteem we refer to the evaluation which the individual makes and customarily maintains with regard to himself: it expresses an attitude of approval or disapproval, and indicates the extent to which the individual believes himself to be capable, significant, successful and worthy. In short, self-esteem is a personal judgment of worthiness that is expressed in attitudes the individual holds toward himself.[1]

But where do the standards we use in judging ourselves come from? Have we learned them from God or from human beings? Have we embraced them in awareness or unexamined? Can we trust those standards? Are they the right ones, the appropriate ones? In sum, are we judging ourselves against the right criteria? And more, how accurately do we judge ourselves against those standards? How accurately do we perceive ourselves? Are we fair and just judges of ourselves? Do we rely on our own opinion, or do we take the opinions of others as the basis for our self-evaluation?

All too often, the values we use in judging ourselves are unexamined: we use them to set a standard, without having much reflected on why, or whether that standard is fair or constructive. And worse, our knowledge of ourselves is patchy or distorted, so that we do not even apply that standard fairly or accurately.

Unexamined Attitudes to Myself

We saw, in the previous chapters, that childhood is a particularly vulnerable time, in relation to forming an understanding of ourselves, of who we are, and how worthy we are. Attitudes to ourselves formed without reflection in early childhood can have a profound influence on us in later life.

The younger the child, the less knowledge he or she has of the world, and the smaller the circle of people whose opinions matter, whose opinions form the earliest basis of self-knowledge and self-evaluation. The younger the child, the more readily he or she will be influenced by the opinions and attitudes of one or two individuals: parents or siblings, perhaps.

We are all, throughout our lives, influenced by other people's opinions and judgments of us. This is a healthy process. To ignore everyone else's opinion completely would lead to a profound isolation, a profound rift in our ability to relate to and respect others. Some psychologists believe that such profound disregard for other people's opinions is the route to madness, or that it is what opens the way to courses of action that are antisocial or even evil.

But healthy development requires us to take possession of ourselves in a way that goes beyond simply accepting the judgments others make on us. Healthy development, as we have seen, requires us to reflect on our understanding of who we are, to pick and choose what will or will not shape our identity or our judgment of self-worth, what we as individuals will value or disregard, what outside opinions we will or will not respect. The young child cannot yet start this process: he or she simply lacks the mental power and knowledge to do it. It is only as we develop and mature that we begin to be able to put other people's opinions of us in a proper perspective: a perspective informed by our own values and reflections. This developmental process lasts a lifetime, as we move toward ever deeper knowledge of ourselves and our values.

Childhood, then, can present us with judgments of ourselves that are dominated by a narrow range of opinion, judgments we cannot reflect on or put in perspective. For example, when we are told that we are bad (or good, for that matter), we simply accept that evaluation without reflection. It may land in our heart and lodge there for many years.

Most of those who work in counseling believe that a great many of the emotional problems individuals suffer in later life stem from the unreflecting acceptance of standards set for us and judgments passed on us in childhood.

For example, the way our parents related to us in infancy sets the stage for how we will relate to others in childhood and in later life, and how we will relate to ourselves. A mother who is consistently sensitive to the needs of her child, who is warm, affectionate, and responsive, creates a child who is secure in his or her affections, and who is confident of love, confident that he or she is *lovable*. Such a child lives in a benign world where it is safe to explore and grow. A father, who is insensitive to the child's needs, or inconsistent in his responses to those needs or in his warmth, creates a child who is anxious and insecure, unsure of love, unsure whether he or she is really lovable. Such a child lives in an unsure world. He or she may be clingy, spending energy seeking reassurance rather than feeling confident to explore. And a mother or a father who is cold and rejecting of the child sends the message that such a child is *not lovable*.

Whatever form of parenting he or she gets, the young child is far too immature to see the parents' behavior in any sort of perspective or to pass any sort of judgment on it. He or she is left, then, with a basic belief about the self that is profound, vital, and unreflected—a core belief that sets the scene for his or her relationship with the self (and with others) perhaps for the rest of life: *I am lovable / I am not lovable.*

The way we are treated as children, whether we were approved of or disapproved of, set hard targets to meet or not, and the very shape of those targets serves to set our first attitudes toward ourselves. We internalize our parents' attitudes to us, and these become our own. We begin to have the same attitude to ourselves that they had. We begin to say the same things to ourselves that they said to us. We also begin to have the same high or low expectations of ourselves that they had of us. It is as if we had made a tape recording of our parents' voices and now we can play it over and over again. And if our parents' attitude toward us was negative, then, our attitude toward ourself will be negative. According to Gershen Kaufman:

> Because we learn to treat ourselves precisely the way we either experienced or observed significant others to do, we learn to shame ourselves, hold ourselves in contempt, blame ourselves, hate ourselves, terrorize ourselves, and even disown a part of ourselves that had been rejected and consistently enough cast away by a parent, whether intentionally or inadvertently. Hence we learn to speak to ourselves, to say the very things subvocally to ourselves which our parents originally said to us.[2]

How many core beliefs do we carry around with us, beliefs set many years ago, in early childhood or in other long-past parts of life? How much power do they still hold over us, over our attitudes toward ourselves? Is it possible to escape from bad judgments of ourselves lodged deep in our hearts, based on long-past and long-irrelevant events?

We shall return to the question of escaping from past judgments later. Here, our focus is on the need to *recognize* just what sorts of judgment we have passed on ourselves, and to begin to explore *why*. What unexamined baggage are we carrying from the past? What unreflecting standards have we adopted as a basis for judging our worth?

Not all damage comes from childhood, of course; any relationship that has exposed us to rejection, denigration, or feelings of low worth has just the same potential to saddle us with negative attitudes toward ourselves. A bad marriage, for example, or a vicious divorce may leave us with very low feelings of worth as we fail in the most intimate task of building a family. Or a brutal workplace, bullying, a society that does not value our work may leave us exposed to feelings of worthlessness.

Such negative attitudes to the self will continue, unless something happens to interrupt them. We can recover from the damaging effects of these negative attitudes. But this only happens when we gain a new view of ourselves, dislodging damaging perceptions. This can happen through discovering new relationships in which others define us in new and more positive ways. It can happen through forming a more aware understanding of ourselves, taking possession of ourselves, exploring our core beliefs about ourselves, and rooting out those that are damaging or untrue. In a spiritual context, we can ask ourselves: *Am I living in the constructive word, the creative house of God? Or am I living in the house of the destructive word?* And if the latter, *Why?*

Applying the Wrong Standards: Success and Failure

One common basis for self-evaluation is in terms of our success or failure in life. This orientation to success and failure is so very deeply rooted in us that it can seem like the obvious and necessary way to judge ourselves. Surely, we need not reexamine *this* core belief.

The Jesuit psychiatrist James Gill wrote:

Sociological research in the United States has found that people evaluate their personal worth not so much by looking at themselves as by measuring their success. This appears true whether the assessment is based on material rewards or spiritual accomplishments. Again, different individuals gauge their degree of success according to different criteria, but each generally learns in early life, from his parents, teachers, and other models, to adopt four principal scales of accomplishment. These include significance, competence, virtue, and power.[3]

Coopersmith expands on these four bases for success in the following way:

> The ability to influence and control others—which we shall term power; the acceptance, attention, and affection of others—significance; adherence to a moral code—virtue; successful performance in meeting demands for achievement—competence.[4]

Our culture is, indeed, very success-oriented. Achievement is everything, and, as Gill commented, we are put under great pressure in childhood and youth to accept success as the defining benchmark in our lives. Succeed in school, or your life will amount to nothing! Succeed in your career, your vocation, your private life, or your life will be a failure! These are the messages that bombard us. But is success really a good basis for self-esteem?

How successful are you, in whichever of the four areas that matters to you? How much of your attitude toward yourself reflects that degree of success or failure? What would happen to your attitude of yourself if all your success were stripped away? What would happen to your attitude of yourself if all your failures were overcome?

The Jewish psychiatrist Bruno Bettelheim survived a Nazi concentration camp. As a prisoner he observed that some individuals seemed to go to pieces very quickly or they began to identify themselves with their persecutors, seeking reassurance from the guards as they tried to reestablish their identity. Other individuals were more robust, more self-contained. They survived better. Those that went to pieces tended to be individuals whose definitions of themselves, whose identity and self-esteem rested more or less entirely on their public success in preprison days: on the titles they had borne, the achievements they could claim and receive public praise for. Those who survived better were those whose identity and self-evaluation survived the stripping away of all those external, public forms of affirmation, of success or failure. Their esteem for themselves was not rooted in success or failure.[5]

In fact, there is scientific evidence that success or failure can never be a complete basis for our self-esteem. Psychologists have discovered that there are two dimensions to our judgments of our own worth.[6] The first is our judgment of how successful we are—whether we are *effective* in meeting our goals in the key areas of achievement. The other dimension is our feeling of whether we are of value or not, that is, what we are *worth*. Society urges us to place our emphasis on success, on being effective, and to value our worth according to our success. And to a degree, that is what we do. Acting effectively makes us feel good about ourselves and value ourselves more positively. Acting ineffectively makes us feel bad about ourselves and devalue ourselves. But this is a very oversimplified picture of the way self-esteem works. For example, an individual who has a very positive attitude of self can cope well with failure—keeping it in perspective and in the proper context—and thereby retain a positive evaluation of self. After all, no one can expect to succeed all of the time! By contrast, an individual with a very negative attitude of self may notice achievement in some task, but instead of taking this as evidence of success and a boost of self-esteem, the achievement is dismissed as "luck" or a "fluke," and a negative attitude of self is retained.

In effect, then, it seems that our basic attitudes of ourselves (attitudes that may come, unexamined, from childhood, or from the past) influence how we interpret success and failure, rather than simply reflecting how successful or unsuccessful we are. It seems that it is our core belief about ourself, whether we have a positive or a negative attitude to ourself, that is vital to self-esteem, rather than success or failure per se.

Spirituality, Success, and Self-Esteem

From a spiritual perspective, success or failure seems irrelevant to my value or worth. The way others treat me is equally irrelevant to my intrinsic worth. We are all precious in God's eyes. Our value comes from *being*, not *doing* or *having*, from my capacity for God, not my worldly status.

We can illustrate that claim with a very famous story: the story of the Good Samaritan, who stopped to help a man who had been mugged. Usually, the emphasis in this story is on the contrast between the Samaritan who stopped to help a stranger and the other passersby who did not. But this story also illustrates the comparison between the Samaritan and the stranger himself; the successful helper and the wounded victim. *Which of these two was worth more?* Surely a key point about this story is that, at least in the Samaritan's eyes, the wounded stranger was worthy of his respect and love, worth helping, even though he was thoroughly beaten and defeated, and rejected by everyone else. The Samaritan in effect treats the stranger with as much respect as himself. And we respect the Samaritan because, deep down, *we accept that he was right.*

It was not the stranger's actions, success, or status that led the Samaritan to respect him—he had been robbed and abandoned and was very far from success at that moment. The Samaritan's respect stemmed from the simple fact of the stranger's *existence*. It was the fact of his *being*, and not anything he might or might not have *done* that made him worthy of respect and love. As Chief Rabbi Jonathan Sacks put it: "Our very dignity as persons is rooted in the fact that none of us—not even genetically identical twins—is exactly like the other. Therefore none of us is replaceable, substitutable, a mere instance of a type. That is what makes us persons, not merely organisms or machines."[7]

Our success-oriented culture moves in fast steps from the observation "I have failed" to the judgment "I am a failure." But failing in any particular endeavor, such as a business venture, a sports competition, or an exam, should be a disappointment and nothing more. In an ideal world, shouldn't we love a child whether or not he or she wins a race, passes an exam, or is popular? Indeed, don't our hearts often go out *more* to a child or a friend who is struggling and beset by problems than to the ones that are comfortable and happy? Love should be about the person, not about his or her successes or failures, status or popularity. We can easily accept this truth *applied to other people*. Isn't it ironic that, often, we do not accept the same basic truth when it comes to loving ourselves? I am just as worthy, just as deserving of respect and love, whether I am a millionaire or bankrupt, whether I am a whizz at passing exams or not, whether I can run a three-minute mile or not, or whether I am bullied, criticized, unpopular or not. Why is this so difficult to accept?

Does Self-Esteem Really Matter?

My self-esteem is the core of my being. The attitude I hold toward myself colors how I interpret my success or failure in the world, and how I interpret and interact with others around me, and with myself, how happy I am. No amount of success in my external world can bring me peace and happiness if I am not at peace in myself and happy with myself. We see the truth of this whenever we see individuals who have all the worldly success, wealth, fame, and adulation anyone could possibly want, but who are not happy, and who have a low opinion of themselves. We see the truth of it when we see individuals who are poor, suffering hardships or privation, perhaps suffering disease or disability, but who are happy and proud of themselves.

Good self-esteem comes from being basically satisfied with

the way I am: accepting myself as I am. To some extent, each individual's acceptance of himself or herself will be personal and unique, reflecting his or her own fundamental values and life experiences. But psychiatrists such as James Sullivan have identified certain common themes underlying good self-esteem. Sullivan identifies three such themes:

- *the need to feel that I am basically good*: I must see myself as noble, attractive, lovable...the opposite of this healthy feeling is the feeling of neurotic guilt or shame
- *the need to feel intelligent*: that I'm capable and adequate for the work I have to do, and that I'm adequate for my situation in life. I need to feel that I can cope and manage—the opposite would be the feeling of inadequacy
- *the need to feel in control of my life*: that I have the moral resources to make my own decisions and pull my own strings—the opposite of this is the neurotic feeling of helplessness, of being trapped.[8]

It is important to notice that what Sullivan is picking out here are *attitudes* toward oneself, and not objective judgments against some worldly scale. I do not need to be Mother Teresa to see myself as "good," nor need I be an academic success to feel adequately clever to cope with my situation, nor free of all constraints to feel in control of my life. We each set the thresholds for acceptance of ourselves, in each of these areas. What I aspire to may be different from what you aspire to in any area, reflecting our unique individuality and experience or, perhaps, reflecting the unexamined standards passed to us by our parents and culture.

Poor self-esteem comes from being dissatisfied with myself: rejecting and criticizing myself as not good enough, not competent enough, not in control of my life. These attitudes need have no basis in objective facts at all: what one individual can happily accept, another will criticize in himself or herself as grossly inadequate. What attitude you have of yourself, whether it is one of positive acceptance or one of negative rejection, will color how you live and experience your life.

For example, the psychologists Morris Rosenberg and Timothy Owens[9] note that all of us face threats to our self-esteem all of the time: other people criticize us or denigrate us, ridicule us, reject us; our flaws and failings may be highlighted by events; we may let ourselves down, and be chagrined or embarrassed. Those with a healthy, high self-esteem will be far less affected by such events, far more able to laugh them off or put them in perspective than those with a negative, low self-esteem. Those with low self-esteem may be reduced to profound depression by criticisms or failures that a healthier individual would simply shrug off. Primed to think badly of themselves, those with low self-esteem are also particularly attuned to noticing information or evidence that confirms their poor opinion of themselves, and to exaggerating such information.

This hypersensitivity to criticism makes people with low self-esteem defensive, protective of themselves. They view life as dangerous, threatening, a disaster waiting to happen. They are less likely to take risks, either with life or with their own personal development than those with a healthier high self-esteem. Where a positive attitude to yourself sets you free to grow and explore, to push your possibilities to the limit—in sum, to be fully alive— a negative attitude to yourself leads to a self-protective withdrawal from challenge, a "safe" course far away from the possibility of failure— in sum, a narrowing and restricting of life.

Low self-esteem is an anxious thing, constantly beset by fear of failure and the conviction that one is inadequate. Lacking self-confidence, the individual with low self-esteem may find any sort of decision too difficult to make, and be trapped in uncertainty, hesitation, doubt. Inevitably, it is a depressing state, a life of misery characterized by pessimism, negative attitudes to life, events and other people.

It's clear that self-esteem really does matter. It affects the whole way we live and experience our lives. And it's also clear that good or bad self-esteem is in our power to control. It comes from the core attitude that we have of ourselves, the core criteria we apply in judging ourselves. It cannot be said often enough that these criteria are not objective, or set in stone, but instead, they are attitudes that we are free to examine and change. Yet so many of us live without exploring those core attitudes, and without exploring where they came from, whether they are justifiable, or appropriate, or constructive.

Examining Our Core Beliefs

All of us suffer attacks on our self-esteem all the time. Whether we are, generally, positive about ourselves or not, we can find ourselves in situations where we are hard pressed to maintain our positive evaluation of ourselves. We can make mistakes that upset us, such as a parent who lets a child down, or a doctor whose efforts fail to save a patient's life, or whose error speeds a death. We can feel like we are not lovable because we have behaved badly, or had thoughts or desires that disturb us, or are contrary to our ideals. We can be challenged by rejection and criticism from other people whose opinions and affections we value.

In such times, we need ways of transcending the harshness of the moment, and ways of retaining our conviction that we are valued, or valuable. How *fair* is the way we view ourselves in such situations? How much reflects the unexamined assumptions of our childhood? How much weight are we putting on success or failure, or on *doing* rather than *being*? Am I judging myself as

I would judge someone else in my position, or am I judging myself more harshly because it is "me"? At such times, there is an urgent need to understand how I view myself, how I judge myself, and what my core beliefs and my core values are in making those judgments.

As a Christian, by faith I know that my true worth comes from God and from my capacity for God. I am precious in his sight! My value as a human being comes, ultimately, from just *being*, from simply being the son or daughter of God. No matter what I have done, no matter what others think of me, my basic humanity deserves and commands respect: *mine, as much as anyone else's*. Coming to believe this is our profoundest spiritual challenge. It is God's challenge to us, and his invitation.

Exercise

Center yourself, using the technique we learned at the end of chapter one.

- Bring yourself to stillness and calm.
- Let yourself feel enfolded in love again: your own love for yourself, and the love of your Higher Power, or God.
- In that loving, safe place, reflect on the way you think about yourself and the way you judge yourself. Where did those standards and attitudes come from? How comfortable are you with the standards you use to judge yourself? Are there any standards that you could let go of or change, right now?
- Now focus again on your breathing.
- And bring yourself gently back to the world.

Like all the exercises that have gone before, this, too, is a very ancient Christian practice. Becoming aware of the negative attitudes we may have of ourselves, and the destructive ways we often judge ourselves, is a crucial step toward freeing ourselves from this negativity: freeing ourselves to grow, spiritually, in a more powerful way.

5

Self-Knowledge, Self-Acceptance

This above all: to thine own self be true,
And it must follow, as the night the day,
Thou canst not be false to any man.

WILLIAM SHAKESPEARE, *HAMLET*

However much my true value and my real nature may rest simply in my *being*, in my *existence* as a human being, or in my capacity for God, it is nonetheless the case that I must also live in and respect the particular human life that is uniquely mine. I must live in, and respect, all the roles that I play, the relationships that I have, the body I inhabit, the personality that is *me*. And to understand who that is, I must take the ideas explored in the first four chapters of this book, and apply them to *me*, exploring my individual past, my individual self.

Christianity has often been associated with denial of this in-dividual human self: denial of its desires, and, particularly, denial and rejection of its propensity for falling below the high standard we feel we ought to live up to; our propensity for selfishness, for meanness, petty-mindedness; our failures of grace, love, charity; even our capacity for wickedness and evil. In other religions, too, there is a tradition of self-denial, self-punishment, and self-rejection.

Is it spiritual to deny the self in this way? Is this what God calls us to? Is denial what our unique individual self can possibly have been made for?

Self, Life, and Denial

The Bible has often been interpreted as a call to repudiate our human selves, to reject and deny ourselves and our "fallen state." For example, negative words such as "I am a worm, and not human" (Psalm 22:6) were taken out of context. Emphasis was put on our sinfulness rather than our grace, and on ourselves as the *fallen* children of Adam rather than as the *redeemed* children of God. This misinterpretation led us to believe that the more we thought of ourselves as bad and unworthy, the more pleasing we were to God.

This belief was a distortion of the biblical message. The very notion of self-denial presupposes self-possession. I cannot deny what I have not yet possessed. Many people have never fully accepted themselves. They have never really accepted that God loves and accepts them just as they are. They have rejected themselves, not out of any religious act of self-denial, but out of a loathing or a dislike of self, a feeling that there is something wrong with "self." To encourage such people to deny themselves would be preaching a masochistic religion to them. Before they can even think about what Jesus means when he says: "If any want to become my followers, let them deny themselves" (Matthew 16:24), they must first be led to a true acceptance of themselves. Most people interpret "self-denial" as shorthand for "I must deny all those tendencies or impulses in myself that would lead me to put myself and my own comfort before others all the time."

To the contrary, the Bible inculcates a very healthy love of self. It is God's invitation to live well, to enjoy life—indeed, to have life more abundantly. It is God's invitation to us to inhabit this human life more fully, more richly, in the light and grace of his Holy Spirit.

Inhabiting my life completely and enjoying life to the fullest is impossible if I reject the vehicle of my existence: my human self. And, in fact, self-rejection changes how I will engage the world, relate to others, and face challenges, opportunities, and risks, as we saw in chapter four. Self-rejection closes down my life, and it closes down my potential to learn and to grow, both as a human being and as one who is growing toward God and toward my fulfilled, spiritual self. Self-rejection is the very antithesis of life in abundance.

A "self-denial" that simply rejects the self in all its reality is no more than *denial*: a refusal to face the truth or to examine fears and doubts about the self. Paradoxically, an honest and truthful acceptance of the self is what provides the foundation for the much healthier form of self-denial advocated by Jesus: the denial of selfishness rather than the self.

God's call, then, is to accept and love ourselves as he loves us. We are called to love our human selves as the vehicle through which we may know God, in whose image we are made. This means accepting and loving the person we are now, the human individual we are today—not some hypothetical person we *might* be one day, nor some partial person, some inner essence divorced from its physical body, its human life. It means *knowing* ourselves as we actually are, accepting all that is within us, and loving ourselves. The commandment is "love your neighbor as yourself" (Matthew 22:39; Mark 12:31; Luke 10:27; Romans 13:9). That commandment is really saying to us, "You should have the same love for your neighbor as you have for yourself" or "the love you have for yourself should be so good that it would be good for your neighbor to love him or her in the same way."

Christianity inculcates a healthy, life-giving love of self. It says, in effect, if you want to love anyone begin by loving yourself. If you cannot love yourself you will not be able to love anyone else.

For many of us, truly knowing and loving ourselves *as we actually are now* rather than as we would like to be or believe we ought to be is one of the greatest spiritual challenges of all.

It is a challenge that can be particularly hard for those who have dedicated their whole lives to God and to the service of others. For example, on being asked how well she knew herself a sister commented: "I prefer not to think about myself. My dedication is to other people." But many great Christians would disagree; for example, Saint Bernard, said:

> You can neither love one you do not know nor possess one whom you have not loved. Know yourself, then, that you may love God; know God, that you may love him. Knowledge of yourself will be the beginning of wisdom, knowledge of God will be the completion, the perfection of wisdom...beware, then...of ignorance of yourself.[1]

On the same theme, the great Scottish mystic Richard of Saint Victor wrote:

> In vain does the eye of the heart, which is not yet fit to see itself, try to see God. First, the man must learn to know his own invisible nature before he presumes to approach the invisible things of God.[2]

And Saint Teresa of Ávila has this to say about the importance of self-knowledge:

However high a state the soul may have attained, self-knowledge is incumbent upon it, and this it will never be able to neglect even if it should desire....Self-knowledge is so important that, even if you were raised right up to the heavens, I should like you never to relax your cultivation of it.[3]

The *Catechism of the Catholic Church* tells us:

Whoever wants to remain faithful to his baptismal promises and resist temptations will want to adopt the *means* for doing so: self-knowledge....[4]

Knowing Myself As I Really Am

My essence, my fundamental nature, is reflected in my capacity for God. But what is my human form?

Actually, human beings are remarkably bad at knowing what we ourselves are like. As Robert Burns, the Scottish poet, said: "Wad some pow'r the giftie gie us, to see ourself as others see us!" All too often, we overlook parts of ourselves that we do not like, do not want to see, or that others have taught us to reject. We may deny problems or patterns of behavior in ourselves; we may focus too harshly on our faults and overlook our virtues. We may fail to recognize ourselves in descriptions others make of us—as in the case of a teacher, who was the only person in the room who did not know that it was she whose quirks were being portrayed in a school play.

Self-knowledge is the root of good self-esteem. It is the *sine qua non* of loving and accepting the self: for how can I love a person I do not know? Many people avoid getting to know themselves because they fear that the self they will discover will be a disappointment, or worse, repulsive. What will be left, if I discover myself to be someone I cannot respect, or someone whose behavior, thoughts, desires, and feelings are contrary to my ideals, or contrary to what I find acceptable? Yet there is no way around the fact that, so long as I avoid knowing myself in my entirety, I am deluding myself. In loving a self I hardly know, I am trapped in loving an illusion that may, at any moment, shatter.

How can we overcome our natural anxieties and engage in a real encounter with ourselves? Getting to know yourself requires patience, effort, and persistence. I am *always* a work in progress, changing as circumstances change, as my knowledge changes, and as I grow in wisdom and experience. Even the effort to know myself will change me. I cannot meet myself *once*, and know myself through and through.

The Dark Side of Personality

Look back over the exercises you have completed so far, working through this book. Perhaps you have made some negative comments on yourself. Perhaps you have criticized yourself for inadequacies in this or that task, or failings here and there in meeting your good intentions. But unless you are very unusual indeed, there will be vast tracts of yourself that remain unexpressed, that are perhaps only shadows in your awareness: things about yourself you would rather not know, and certainly do not want to say.

The fact is that there is far more to each of us than meets the eye. However much of our individual personality may reflect innate dispositions, a very great deal reflects the culture in which we live. Many thoughts and actions that were perfectly acceptable in human history are unacceptable now, such as enslaving another against his or her will, ritual murder, or cannibalism, to name just a few extreme examples. Yet our biological selves have not changed. The potential to think those thoughts and to perform those actions remains a part of our biological heritage, as is sadly evident from any television newscast or any newspaper. It is our culture, our collective, and our individual pursuit of spiritual values that have made such things unacceptable.

As we develop, we foster those aspects of our potential personality that are acceptable and approved by our culture, and we suppress those impulses and thoughts that are not acceptable. The great analyst of this process was Sigmund Freud, who argued that we consciously experience only a small part of our desires, impulses, and thoughts. The rest, the things that are socially (or personally) unacceptable, we repress into our subconscious minds. Here, according to Freud, such thoughts and feelings may foment, soaking up our energies as we strive to repress and deny them; or sneaking past our defenses in disguise to affect our conscious lives one way or another, as when, for example, some forbidden sexual urge is "sublimated," its native energy being channeled to fuel some more acceptable pursuit.

Should we search out these repressed, subconscious thoughts and feelings? Psychiatrists in the psychoanalytic tradition would say that we should, especially where our efforts to defend ourselves against these unconscious impulses disrupt our ordinary lives. But such efforts to know the subconscious are, by their very nature, disturbing, difficult, and dangerous.

Is my behavior distorted by subliminal thoughts or by ideas that are unacceptable to me. Are such thoughts disturbing my ability to see myself as the person I would like to be? And how should I react, if this is so? Is this really a part of me that I need to know about? Psychologists disagree on the answers to such questions.

A friend of mine, a psychologist much given to reflection on this sort of thing, described herself recently as having, for a fleeting moment, been aware of "a violent urge to bite the obstreperous and difficult woman behind the counter at the store or difficult clerk behind the register, to bite her firmly on her fleshy arm."

Biting a shop assistant is clearly completely unacceptable, particularly for an educated woman over forty. The woman in question might have been profoundly shocked at herself for even entertaining the notion; she might have reacted by thinking: *What an awful person I must be, to even have entertained such a terrible thought. Maybe I am not a healer, after all, as I thought, as people imagine, but a dangerously violent maniac?* Discovering ourselves in some unacceptable thought or act can be deeply disturbing. It can horrify us, or lead us to reject ourselves and recoil inward, away from that which defines who we really are. But is this the right reaction?

In fact, my friend simply laughed at her impulse to bite. Who better than a psychologist to know that we may *all* have dark and secret impulses, dark and secret sides of our characters hidden even from ourselves? Needless to say, she has never been known to bite (well, not since her second birthday, anyway), and resisted the impulse on that day, too! She recognized this dark impulse for what it was, a fleeting response dredged up from infant memories, and rejected it as inconceivable as a course of action. The point is *if we do not act on them, if we reject them, how can such thoughts, however bad, shame us?* Isn't our very reaction of horror and repudiation of such antisocial thoughts or acts, in fact, a source for pride? Note: it is the bad thought that we reject. It should not be ourselves. And, we have to remind ourselves, we are not our thoughts. We are not our good thoughts, and we are certainly not our bad thoughts.

Psychologists have shown that the difference between the normal, healthy population and those behind bars is not a difference in the degree to which we entertain unacceptable fantasies—such as robbing a bank, having a torrid affair, driving at 120 mph, or even sailing off to sea and leaving someone else to sort out all the domestic crises—but rather, our stability is determined by the extent to which we act on such thoughts. As it turns out, we all indulge in such thoughts. Perhaps all need to acknowledge this dark tendency, and to accept that it is part of what it is to be human. Ultimately, the difference between the normal population and the mad or bad is that normal people do not *act* on these dark thoughts.

Sometimes, of course, the darker side of ourselves is so strong that it worms its way into our conscious lives in a more direct and disruptive way. Understanding these repressed thoughts and motives can then become a more important part of understanding who we are and how we behave. We may, for example, act to disrupt a friendship between two others, telling ourselves that we are acting in their best interests, when, in fact, we are really motivated by a jealousy that is too unacceptable to us to admit, and so it is repressed and denied.

Does it help to recognize the darker impulses of a human mind or the flaws we would rather hide away, even from ourselves? The answer depends on what the result of this knowledge will be, or what we will do with it. If it will just become another stick to beat myself with, then ignorance may well be better. But if I can *know* myself to be someone who can, for example, fantasize biting strangers in a shop, *know* myself as someone who has deliberately rejected this urge, and know that I am healthy and lovable *anyway*. Then my picture of what it is to be human and what it is to be the *particular* person that I am is enriched. And in coming to understand myself in this richer, deeper, and more tolerant way, do I not also become more tolerant of foibles and peculiarities in *you*?

Admitting That We Have Virtues

OK. We all have a dark side. When we set out to discover our "true" self, there is a temptation to focus on this dark side, to say: *Well, I know the good news, I suppose I'd better find out the bad.* But the fact is that we are just as bad, sometimes worse, at admitting our good features as we are at admitting our bad features. We can fail to know ourselves just as much through ignoring our virtues as through ignoring our vices.

Why is it so hard for so many of us just to come out and say, "Actually, I am someone special, someone brave, clever and compassionate, someone who makes a difference to other people's lives"? We were taught to be modest. We were taught not to boast. We learn, early, that people prefer those who understate their strengths rather than those who flaunt them or exaggerate them. And, of course, there is something in this lesson; something we think is right; something we pass on to our children. We do not boast foolishly about our virtues. Neither should we foolishly deny them.

One can take modesty too far. Suppose I happen to have a particular talent. For example, lets say that I am a gifted doctor. An unusual and rare emergency develops for which I have little or no experience. Another person's life is in the balance. Is it right to modestly deny my abilities and do nothing? Or should I come forward and say, "Although I have never done this before, I have a talent that exceeds anyone else here, and I will do my best to solve the problem." Most of us would think a doctor who let modesty rule in such a situation was wrong, or selfish. We would prefer that doctor to make the effort, even if it failed. We would rather that he or she was honest in admitting talent, knowledge, and gifts.

Of course, most of us are not doctors, and few doctors ever face such a dilemma. But it is a mistake to think that our own personal gifts amount to nothing. Not all contributions to life involve drama or grand gestures. For example, here is a story I heard from a friend:

My great-auntie Mary never left the town she was born in, except for a couple of holidays. She never married. She never left her mother's home: she lived with her parents until each died, and then lived on alone in their home. She had no formal education or qualifications. She had contracted a crippling disease at the age of twelve and she had to leave behind the things that once defined her as normal. From a modern, materialistic perspective, her whole life was narrow, closed off, and dull. But when she died, a hundred or more people came to her funeral! Too many to fit into the small church. The crowds at her funeral testified to a greatness behind her otherwise drab appearance. I began to understand when, on the morning of the funeral, I went to two shops in the town. The first was a florist, to fetch flowers. The florist had prepared far more than I had asked and would not be paid. She took my hand, and told me how much Mary would be missed. The second was a shoe shop; my small son had lost his shoe that morning and could hardly go barefoot to a funeral. They fitted the shoes for him, but the manager would not take my money: it was his tribute to Mary. The fact was that Mary possessed the rare and precious gifts of listening and caring. That is, she had the gift of saying the healing word. Just living in her own community and using her gifts with humility, she had changed how people saw and related to one another. She had been the heart of the community. I think she knew this. I hope that she did.

All of us may have gifts that could enrich our world. Not to acknowledge them is to deny a fundamental part of ourselves. Denying such gifts may mean that we fail to use them. What strengths, what gifts, what virtues do I have? How can I truly know myself, if I do not acknowledge these gifts in pure honesty?

Recognizing Core Beliefs About the Self

One area in which it is, without doubt, beneficial to bring long-hidden things into consciousness is in the area of the core beliefs that we as individuals hold about ourselves.

Do I, at bottom, like and respect myself? Am I basically positive about myself and glad to be me? Am I acceptable to myself? Or do I, at my core, dislike and devalue myself? Am I basically negative about myself, making the best of an unlucky draw in life? Do I reject myself?

This basic attitude toward the self has nothing to do with success, power, or status, as we saw in earlier chapters. One can be rich beyond imagination, the object of adulation across the world, beautiful, or successful, and still be unhappy, self-destructive, and self-rejecting. One can be poor, unsuccessful, ugly, and yet be entirely happy and self-accepting. Our attitudes to ourselves are not a pure reflection of our worldly success and failure. Rather, these core attitudes toward ourselves shape how we interpret and experience success or failure in our lives.[5] Core attitudes toward ourselves come first.

As we saw in the last chapter, our core attitude to our self, whether we feel lovable or not, may be primed in early infancy, learned from our mother's reactions to us. It may be shaped through some later loss or rejection: through a father who abandons us, as he abandons his marriage, for example, or a lover who turns against us. It may be lodged deep in our hearts or our unconscious minds, which makes it hard to bring out, examine, and acknowledge. How can I come to recognize this attitude toward myself? How can I come to understand how it colors my interpretation of life? How, if it is a negative attitude, can I change it?

Recognizing that we hold a core attitude toward ourselves

that is negative and damaging is harder than you might imagine. So often, we take the judgment we have made of ourselves as "objective" to be a reflection of fact in the real world, when, actually, it is anything but that. For example, two sixteen-year-old boys from two different families received their exam results on the same day. The first was delighted, his family was delighted, and the boy was endorsed as a successful member of his school and his family. As such, he was identified as a person with a rosy future. The second boy was horrified. His family was distressed. He was cast as a failure, as having blighted his chances for the future. Ironically, these two boys had exactly *the same* grades, and exactly *the same* chances for the future. The judgment made of them by others and by themselves was in no way objective. It was the subjective reflection of expectations set by their families: expectations that were, in fact, completely arbitrary in either case.

It is easy, in this example of the two schoolboys, to see the constructive and useful attitude of the first family, and the destructive and hurtful attitude of the second. Instinctively, we are critical of the second family, and we want to reject the standards they set for judging their child. But when we have negative attitudes toward ourselves, very often, we are in the same position as the second boy: we have blindly accepted a standard that is not only destructive, but entirely arbitrary.

How constructive and nurturing was your family, schooling, upbringing, church or faith community? These questions can be hard to ask, and hard to answer. We shy away from the risk of hurt from asking, honestly, how well we were loved as children. We do not always want to know the answer. But knowing where I have come from and how I came to be as I am is an important element of knowing who I am. Did I grow up confident that I was lovable and worthy of love? Or did I grow up uncertain of love, feeling that I was unlovable, and not worthy of love? Who gave me this message, this basic attitude toward myself? Can I now, as an adult, see that such a message is more a reflection of the person who sent it than of me? How wonderful, how lucky, if the message we received was good! For that good message told us the truth: every young child is lovable, and every child should grow up knowing it. But if the message we received was bad, we should see it for what it is and reject it.

The idea that we are lovable (or not) may be implanted in infancy. But childhood teaches us other things about our worth, too: it teaches us how to judge ourselves, by showing us how vital we are to our family and others.

As in the example of the two schoolboys, negative attitudes to the self are often associated with perfectionism. The perfectionist cannot accept himself or herself as worthy, if the high standards he or she sets are not met. Perfectionism is, profoundly, dysfunctional: judged by a standard that demands perfection, we are almost bound to fail. The perfectionist tends to think dichotomously, seeing things in black and white, and overgeneralizing, so that one failure may be mistaken as evidence of constant or complete failure. As Wilkie Au and Noreen Cannon say: "Perfectionism…is that voice in us that says we have not done enough and therefore do not deserve to feel satisfied."[6] Never satisfied, the perfectionist pays a high price in relentless self-criticism, a state that robs them of spiritual peace, psychological balance, and even physical health.

The psychologist Karen Horney describes the perfectionist as prey to what she calls "the tyranny of the shoulds": we command ourselves to achieve, to behave thus, and so we believe that we *ought* to do things, things that really are often a matter of taste or preference rather than a matter of moral imperative as the perfectionist takes them to be. The perfectionist believes that he or she *must* do certain things (achieve or avoid criticism and so on) to be worthy, where another person might see those things as attractive, but not imperative. This can include anything from succeeding in work to achieving self-improvement, love, or happiness.

Where does perfectionism come from? Matthew McKay and Patrick Fanning suggest that certain styles of parenting can leave a child with a tendency toward perfectionism: parenting that directly mislabels matters of taste, preference, safety, or good judgment as moral imperatives; parenting that takes bad behavior to indicate a bad character; parenting that is full of negative messages, forbidding gestures; parenting that is inconsistent in its negative evaluations, that leaves the child uncertain of the rules; parenting that uses anger or withdrawal to reinforce a negative message.[7]

Many people with poor self-esteem are perfectionists. Letting go of such an attitude to the self is difficult. The need to achieve or strive for perfection is so deeply ingrained that letting go it can look like letting go of direction, purpose, and commitment: all threats to the perfectionist way of thinking. The easygoing person can look downright sloppy to the driven perfectionist—not something he or she would want to be.

Yet it is possible to let go of a perfectionist approach to life. The example of the two schoolboys gives us a clue as to how perfectionist tendencies develop. The perfectionist judgement of the second boy that made his effort *not good enough,* where a different view was not only possible, but more constructive, surely give us pause to reflect on the dangers and inappropriateness of perfectionism. "Ah yes!" the perfectionist may reply, "but probably the exam results weren't good enough, and the family was right to criticize and worry." In fact, both of these boys had taken eight exams. Both had achieved the highest possible grade in six of these and dropped only one grade in the remaining two. Both had exceeded the achievement needed for their chosen courses by a comfortable margin. The absurdity of the contrast between the two families, the absurdity of the perfectionist stance, is clear.

Put in context, isn't our own perfectionism often equally absurd and unnecessary?

The core attitudes we hold toward ourselves, and about how we should be judged, can either energize or drain us. These powerful beliefs may well have entered our lives early in childhood, not because they reflect any value we may actually have or any values we would actually want to endorse, but because of the accidents of personality in those who happened to parent us. Living by such beliefs for a lifetime without ever examining them leaves us at the mercy of chance. This is no basis for building a strong self, a self that is adequate for a lifetime of challenges and setbacks, a self that is adequate for its journey toward God. And this is true, whether the attitudes I hold toward myself are negative or positive, or whether they are perfectionist or balanced.

So long as we do not understand where our core attitudes toward our self come from, we are vulnerable to misunderstanding them, and to mistaking an attitude for an objective fact, for example. And so long as we simply accept these attitudes without reflection, we are vulnerable to assaults on our self-esteem. These may be continuous, coming from applying damaging standards that our conscious mind would reject, where our core attitude is negative. Or they may be more occasional, where our core attitude is positive. If I misunderstand the roots of my feeling of being lovable, for example, I may lose it if circumstances that I think are relevant change. If I feel myself to be lovable *simply* because people love me, for instance, do I retain that confidence if, one day, there is no one left who loves me? Coming to understand my own core attitudes toward myself, and where these came from, is a key step on my path toward self-knowledge and self-acceptance.

Self-Acceptance

As we have examined our secret selves, and examined the core attitudes we hold toward ourselves, we have come to some surprising conclusions.

Our attitudes toward ourselves are just that: attitudes, reflecting the arbitrary attitudes of those who parented us. There is no rock-solid basis for these attitudes; we are not lovable just because someone loved us, anymore than we are unlovable just because we are not loved. The standards we judge ourselves by are also arbitrary; we could set them higher or lower with equal justification, as other people do. Where we set our sights is arbitrary within a purely human context.

How, then, in such an arbitrary world, am I to decide between one set of values and another, between one way of valuing myself and another? It is here that the spiritual dimension comes in with force: we accept ourselves, absolutely, because we *exist*, and because we exist in the image of God. There are no other conditions for self-acceptance whatsoever, from a spiritual perspective.

The Zen mantra, "What I am is enough, what I have is enough," is typical of the way all the great religions approach this question. As Guardini says, self-acceptance is the foundation of our existence, the "root of all things."[8] And this must be a complete, absolute self-acceptance: we must accept ourselves as God accepts us—as precious in his eyes.

The Fellowship of Alcoholics Anonymous, which is the archetype for successful self-help support groups, discovered the liberating and healing power of self-acceptance. This is how they express it:

> ...acceptance is the answer to all my problems today. When I am disturbed today, it is because I find some person, place or thing, or situation—some aspect of my life—

unacceptable to me, and I can find no serenity until I accept that person, place or thing or situation as being exactly the way it should be at the moment. Nothing, absolutely nothing happens in God's world by mistake. Until I could accept my alcoholism, I could not stay sober; until I accept life completely on life's terms, I cannot be happy. I need to concentrate not so much on what needs to be changed in the world as on what needs to be changed in me and in my attitudes.

For Alcoholics Anonymous, this absolute acceptance of self, and of the present, rests in an absolute faith in what they call a "higher power": what Christian believers call God.

For the Christian, positive beliefs about the self come from God's word. It is God who reveals to us our worth and value. Beginning with the revelation that we have been made in God's image, the Bible gives us many reasons for accepting, utterly, that we are valued. Despite all our failures and sinfulness we are precious in God's sight (Isaiah 43:4). God can never forget us (Isaiah 49:15). He assures us that there is no need to be afraid "for I am with you" (Isaiah 43:5). When we are overcome with a sense of our own sinfulness or guilt, he says, "a new heart I will give you, and a new spirit I will put within you" (Ezekiel 36:26). God's Holy Spirit teaches us to pray, "I praise you, for I am fearfully and wonderfully made" (Psalm 139:14). In the Gospel, Jesus assures us that "God so loved the world that he gave his only Son, so that everyone who believes in him may not perish, but may have eternal life" (John 3:16), and that he came so that we might have "life, and have it abundantly" (John 10:10), indeed, that we might have "eternal life" (John 10:28). Scripture reassures us that we are "what he has made us, created in Christ Jesus" (Ephesians 2:10), and that we are "the body of Christ" (1 Corinthians 12:27), and "a temple of the Holy Spirit" (1 Corinthians 6:19). When

Christ comes again we shall be like him, because we shall see him as he really is. If we believe in God, believe in his word, then we have here the ultimate grounds for valuing ourselves, the only grounds we need: *we are precious in his sight.*

Just As I Am

Letting go of extrinsic standards and criteria for judging whether I am worthy or not is liberating. I am fine, lovable, and sufficient just as I am! The burden of effort to be good enough to qualify as an acceptable human being falls away. The worry about whether I have done enough to qualify falls away.

The relief of truly accepting this truth, that I am fine just as I am, can be enormous. This is as it should be: there is no entrance test to being human. Every human life is precious and worthy of dignity, respect, and love. And, as we will see, the first condition for growth in the future is the acceptance of oneself in the present.

Progressively, institutions of international law and justice, of human rights, have embraced this ancient spiritual truth. As the sociologist Grace Davie says: "It is important to stress one point in particular: the shared religious heritage of Western Europe as one of the crucial factors in the continent's development—and possibly in its future—and the influence of this heritage on a whole range of cultural values."[9] The values of human rights and the dignity of every human person were not always recognized, even by great philosophers like Aristotle or Plato. Without being able to ground human dignity in the creative love of God we will always find it difficult to act on the belief that all human beings are equal.

We grow in grace *because* grace makes us good and *because* we are precious, *not* in order to become so. We grow in grace because, given a chance, such growth is our nature: that is, it is in our nature to be the image of God. That is why Jesus can say to us, "Be merciful, just as your Father is merciful" (Luke 6:36). When Jesus looks at us he believes that we are actually capable of being like God. What a fantastically high opinion Jesus has of each one of us! He believes that, as we live with compassion in our hearts, we live and grow toward the divine.

Exercise

Center yourself, using the technique we learned at the end of chapter one.

- Bring yourself to stillness and calm.
- Let yourself feel enfolded in love, as before.
- Open your mind to all the good, all the talent, all the virtue that is in you; all the love and compassion of which you are capable. Perhaps you would find it helpful to pick out one particular thing to focus on.
- Feel how special and wonderful that is.
- Let your whole heart rejoice in the gifts you have. Feel as much joy and celebration from those gifts as you can.
- Now focus again on your breathing.
- And come gently back to the world.

Again, this is an old Christian practice. We rejoice, and give thanks to God for our lives, our individuality, and all the good things that are in and around us.

6

The Grace
of Forgiveness

To err is human; to forgive, divine.
ALEXANDER POPE

Reflecting on our own personal past as we seek to know ourselves better, and on the events of history and the mores of society that have contributed to the world we live in, it is easy to find many causes of resentment, anger, bitterness. We may find many bases for a sense of grievance, and we may also find many areas of unresolved hurt and pain. Such feelings may distort and dominate our lives in subtle or more obvious ways. Is it better to hang on to such emotions or to let them go? To incubate grievance and hurt, or to forgive? How much damage does it do to us, emotionally, physically, or spiritually, bearing such grudges?

Incubating Grievance

Bad things happen in every life. People hurt us, deliberately or otherwise. We let ourselves down, and sometimes hurt ourselves. Things go wrong for us. The pain of the hurt is bad enough when it first happens. Unfortunately, we can allow that pain to continue long after the event that caused it.

It may happen, for example, that your best friend told a lie about you in 1963. That was a very painful discovery. You had a right to be hurt and angry. But would it be reasonable still to feel those things over forty years later, in 2005? Would it be reasonable to feel those emotions when the events are long past, and the friend responsible may even be dead? Yet, so often, we do feel hurts and resentments, many, many years after the events that originally provoked those feelings. Divorced persons may nurse a grievance against their former spouse, for example, thirty years or more after their divorce. Or they may remain bitter for many years about being passed over for promotion, even if they actually received the promotion shortly after the initial rejection. Or, a person may continue to blame his or her parents for poor parenting, thereby carrying emotional baggage through to the end of their own life.

Our propensity to hang on to pain and resentment for years after the event is a curious thing. We have a grievance, and instead of letting it go and getting on with life, we feed and foster it, allowing all the damage of the original hurt to attack us again and again, year after year. We rehearse and repeat the grievance, letting it interfere with life in the present day. Doing this can seem justified or inevitable: *Haven't I, after all, suffered a grievous wrong? How can I be expected just to forget about it?* But this way of thinking is absurd. The hurtful event is long gone; it is in the past. We wish we had never suffered that hurt in the first place. How, then, can it make sense to put ourselves through the same hurt, over and over again, in our memory and imagination? Who is damaged by that but ourselves? What is gained?

Nevertheless, we do harbor and feed hurts. We create what Fred Luskin describes as a "grievance story" that nurtures our hurt.[1] This is the story that we repeat over and over. The grievance story is not the original hurt. But we tend to forget that. We forget that, as well as the actual event, there is the perspective in which we see the event and the meaning that we give to it. The event is the objective reality, the thing that occurred. The perspective is the personal vision in which I see the event. And the meaning I give to the event is determined, not by the event itself but by my perspective on it.

For example, if my friend agrees to come to supper but does not turn up, I may well be upset or even angry. My perspective on this is likely to be that he does not want to see me, and that he cannot even be bothered to let me know. I feel hurt, offended, and rejected. I have a grievance. But if I later discover that he crashed his car on the way to me, and that instead he was in the hospital with a concussion, then my perspective changes, and the meaning I give to the event changes with it.

As we tell the story of a grievance, we forget that we are not reciting objective facts, but giving our own perspective and interpretation of events. And it is this perspective, and the meaning we place upon it, that determine what effect a hurtful event will have on our lives.[2] If nothing happens to change our perspective, or change the meaning we give to the hurtful event, we may be trapped with this hurt for decades.

Reexamining Old Grievances

The grievances we nurse the longest are those where the perspective we have on the original event, and the meaning we give to it, most closely wounds us. We take it to heart. But how often is this reaction based on misunderstandings of either ourselves, the other party, or the event itself?

We may take events very personally, when we should not do so. For example, John and Fred had been good friends for years, but when John got a promotion that Fred had set his heart on, Fred refused to speak with John. Not only that, to this day he tells people how his former friend pulled a fast one on him and got the job that he should have had. As a result, naturally, John is upset in return. He is particularly distressed that Fred seems to believe that in some way he acted unjustly by allowing his name to go forward for the promotion. He is also angry that Fred keeps telling all his friends that he pulled a fast one on him. John feels helpless in the face of all Fred's indignation and bitterness. He finds that he is giving more and more time to thinking about Fred and the lies he is spreading, and he is aware, too, that he is now telling his own story about Fred. If Fred thinks he has a grievance, John is now certain that he, too, with much greater reason, has a grievance. Both men are taking what happened too personally. Neither can stand back from his own very personal pain and reaction to events, and see that, in fact, people will, even at a risk to friendship, and without intending to hurt one another, go for the same job. Or that when someone has been passed over for a promotion he or she may very well feel deep resentment, anger, and jealousy, and take this out on the person who got the promotion. Acknowledging these commonplace facts would put both men's grievances in a new perspective, a perspective that would defuse pain and hurt, but neither is able to do it. How often do we make the same mistake?

Having construed an event as a deliberate attack or effort to hurt us, we then blame the perpetrator for our own emotional reaction to that event. Again, this is a misunderstanding of the situation and of ourselves. There is an important difference between holding someone responsible for what *they* have done and holding them responsible for how *you* feel. What they did is, properly, their responsibility. How you feel is, actually, *your* responsibility. And this obvious fact is true, whether or not the person who has hurt us meant to or not. There is no automatic connection between any attack on us and our emotional response to it. If someone steals my wallet, for example, I may feel rage and anger at the person, or I may feel pity for the need that drove that person to steal. It is perfectly correct to say, "It was that person who stole my wallet," and, "I hold that individual responsible for that act." But how I respond to that act, whether I am vengefully angry or compassionate, or accept the fact with neutral equanimity, *is entirely my own responsibility*. How long I go on harboring that feeling, when the act is long past, is also my own responsibility. This point is so obvious when we reflect on it, but how often do we make this mistake ourselves?

Other grievances come from our failure to recognize that another person is different from us, has different values and expectations, different ways of behaving, and that he or she is perfectly entitled to those differences. We have no right to compel another person to do or say or be what we think he or she should do or say or be; other people have a right to be themselves. Forgetting this fact is the cause of so many grievances that often occur between parent and child, for example. How often do parents feel anger and resentment and hurt when a child refuses to live the sort of life the parents wanted for him or her? The parents nurse a grievance because the child has hurt them, let them down, or "failed." But this grievance is entirely unfair: parents have the right to *hopes*, but not to *demands*. The parents may fairly feel disappointed, but anger and resentment are inappropriate; children have no obligation to live by their parents' will, and have not done anything wrong in wishing to be themselves and live their own lives. The parents' grievance comes only from their failing to recognize how illegitimate their expectations were in the first place. It is not only parents who make this mistake: husbands and wives, friends, or colleagues may also fail to honor each other's right to be themselves. A husband may, for example, expect his wife to live up to his own standards and values, and blame her when she does not. He is blaming her for being a failed version of himself, which he had no right to expect of her. Instead, he should allow her to be her own version of herself. How often are the grievances I nurture due to making this sort of mistake?

We may blame someone—a parent, say, or a lover, or a priest, or a politician—for not being the person we needed them to be, not treating us as we feel we should have been treated, or holding them responsible for failing to live up to standards we have set for them: standards that they never themselves aspired to, never understood, and perhaps never had the ability or the experience to achieve. We demand perfection in that other person and feel aggravated when we do not find it. We prefer to blame the person for this "fault" rather than saying, "Perhaps they did the very best they could for me with what practical, psychological, or spiritual resources were available to them, and with what understanding was available to them." This realization can be enormously liberating: the hurts we have suffered were *not* intended. They were consequences of the human condition and not the deliberate attacks that we perceived them to be. But how often we fail to achieve this insight, or fail to embrace the tolerance for others that it implies!

The History of a Grievance

What happens when we have a grievance, when we harbor a profound hurt? A number of stages have been identified in this experience. Not everyone will go through every stage, or start in the same place. One may go back and forth between stages, covering old ground. Different writers have identified different stages, or named the same stages differently, but here is one outline of the history of a grievance.

(1) *Denial:* We may deny that the hurtful event has happened at all, and try to shove it out of sight in our unconscious mind. A wife may refuse to acknowledge the evidence that her husband is unfaithful, for example, or a child may deny that his or her father is a brutal drunk. Even when we are forced to acknowledge the event we remain in denial, such as one might find when an unfaithful spouse seeks a divorce. The abandoned spouse may deny the hurt, shrugging it off, claiming that it is "over and done with" or "just so much water under the bridge of life." The unloved child may say: "I don't care!" Denial allows us to carry on without dealing with the problem or our wounds, and this can feel safer than admitting how vulnerable we are. But this leaves the pain unacknowledged, undealt with, lurking there in our subconscious mind, ready to distort our life.

(2) *Self-blame:* What sort of people blame themselves when someone else has hurt them? The answer seems to be, *anyone of us.* When bad things happen to us, we have a strong tendency to think, "If only I had done things differently, this would not have happened. If only I had been a better wife," for example, "he would not have left! If only I had been a better child, daddy would not have been so angry! If only I had prepared better, worn a different tie, or played golf with the manager, I would not have been passed over. I would have gotten John's job! If only I had left earlier to catch the bus, I would not have been mugged, or would not have been raped walking home." Self-blame, like denial, makes us feel safer. "If I could have prevented this woe by behaving differently, I can prevent it from ever happening to me again. I can keep myself safe in the future by doing things differently."

But this self-blame is another form of denial; by blaming ourselves, we are denying that bad things can happen to us whatever we do. The truth is the world *is* a dangerous place. We are *never* responsible for an unfaithful spouse, a brutal father, or a mugging. Adultery, brutality, theft, and rape are not actions forced on our assailants, no matter what we do. These are decisions made by those persons, and they have nothing to do with us. Bad things happen, things that are entirely beyond our control. Blaming ourselves is not a healthy solution.

(3) *Feeling like a victim:* Understanding that something bad has happened to me, something that was grossly unfair, wrong, or horrible is a healthy step in many ways. It is the first step toward acknowledging, honestly, what has actually happened, and that it was *wrong*. Until we do this, we cannot begin to come to terms with events, or to put them in perspective. But seeing ourselves as the helpless and innocent victim of a malign fate can lure us toward self-pity: "It is all so unfair that I have suffered such damage and now I am so unfairly handicapped in life." Such a self-perception can lead us to wallow in pain, to nurse our grievance, to use it to excuse all manner of failures to deal with the problem, failures to grow past it. Focusing on myself as a victim encourages a distorted view of life: "Yes, I have been unfairly wounded. But am I the only one? Is my hurt greater than anyone else's? Is it large enough to justify my overwhelming absorption in my pain?" Taking victimization too seriously, too much out of the context of what other human beings have suffered, and choosing to live the rest of my life as a victim are decisions that lock us into pain and cut us off from growth. The temptation is strong! But psychologists are discovering that, often, events that traumatized, wounded, and changed our lives in ways we did not anticipate or want can be the key to new growth, new perspectives, and new life, if only we let ourselves grow beyond the victim stage. Great examples of

this are Nelson Mandela, robbed of decades of his life in the name of political repression, but refusing to be a victim; or the parents of Megan Kanka, the seven-year-old that was raped and killed by an unknown assailant. Instead of being totally victimized, they fought back by establishing a legal warning system—known as Megan's Law—to protect other children.

(4) *Indignation:* People like these refused to be victims. They got mad, not sad. Indignation at what has been so unjustly done to you energizes you for action. It releases your healthy anger from repression. Many of us deny our anger or unconsciously repress it. We may even believe that anger in itself is bad or sinful. But anger can be a good emotion. Anger directed at vengeance is bad; anger directed at injustice is good. Indignation is a healthy step on our path to wholeness. We can reject passive victimization and embrace an active effort to redress the wrong. Clearly, this is healthier than anything that has gone before. But anger is not enough to heal us from our hurts. And getting stuck at a stage where our primary response is anger can be as destructive as anything else; we turn into angry people fuelled by rage, ready to release it on a hair trigger. Sometimes hurt people, who have discovered their anger, remain stuck in it for years. Their anger becomes aggression and their behavior unacceptable, even to their friends. They end up not only hurt, but friendless.

(5) *Survivors:* Nelson Mandela and the parents of Megan Kanka are not merely indignant; they are survivors (and much more). The survivor begins to make the discovery that, despite the hurt and rejection, life is beginning to have a new meaning and purpose. Life is no longer defined and prescribed by the hurts of the past; life is open to the future and it is up to oneself to make a good future. The wounded person discovers that life is still good and worth living. "For one thing, in the survivor stage you spend

more and more time *looking ahead toward health instead of back toward your pain.*"[3] You begin to realize that despite everything that happened to you, you are still alive, still in charge of your own life, and now you want to get your life back under your own control. You recognize that living in denial or self-blame, in victimhood or indignation, was not a healthy lifestyle. The hurts and wounds of the past were real, but they belong to the past. You do not have to bring them into the future. The survivor draws a line in the sand and proclaims that the resentments, grudges, bitterness, and unforgiveness will not pass that line. Negative emotions and reactions will not be part of the future that is opening up, or they will not be part of what defines me and my life.

> Although you may have thought this before, in the survivor stage you actually do it. After years of merely responding to the people and circumstances that you happened to encounter, you take back the reins that you handed over to fate and play an active role in determining your own destiny. You become an actor instead of a reactor; a player in the game of life rather than a spectator watching from the sidelines while life passes you by.[4]

(6) *Integration:* One day, often without our expecting it, we wake up and realize that the miracle has happened, we have let go of the pain and the resentment and the rage from our grievance. We have forgiven. Something has happened inside us. C. S. Lewis wrote to his friend Malcolm: "Last week while at prayer, I suddenly discovered—or felt as if I did—that I had forgiven someone I had been trying to forgive for over thirty years."[5] Forgiveness happens within us before we can offer it to others. At the stage of integration, it is not a question of trying, or forcing, oneself to forgive. Rather, it is the discovery that in some mysterious way

we have already forgiven. All the emotional baggage that bound us to the past hurt has been jettisoned. You can look back at the hurt with new insight. As Rowan Williams, Archbishop of Canterbury, wrote: "If forgiveness is liberation, it is also a recovery of the past in hope, a return of the memory, in which what is potentially threatening, destructive, despair-inducing in the past is transfigured into a ground of hope."[6] As I accept my past, and everything that has happened to me in the past, I can accept myself just as I am in the present in a new and healing way. In accepting yourself unconditionally in the present, you can also accept the hurts of the past that contributed in their own way to how you are in the present. The truth is that you were always *more* than your hurt. At the integration stage you discover the "more," and you do so in a way that would seem to be totally foolish to a person in the victim stage—for this you can be grateful. You no longer try to banish the person who hurt you from your life. You now accept that that person has had a role in your life history and you want to keep your history intact. In fact, you are now so healed within that you may be ready for reconciliation with the person who hurt you if that person is ready to reciprocate. But your forgiveness does not depend on reconciliation. Your forgiveness is now unconditional. Your forgiveness is something that has happened within you, and the fact that the other person is not willing to be reconciled in no way limits or restricts the quality of your forgiveness. Now, even if he or she tells you to "stuff your forgiveness" you are still forgiving. The reason should now be obvious. Forgiveness is not what he or she deserves, nor is it a duty that you owe or a moral obligation that you are under. It is your inalienable right as a person to protect your personal dignity, and to heal your wounds. Philip McGraw sums it up well when he writes:

The reason I believe forgiveness is such an important element is that without it you are almost inevitably destined to a life marred by anger, bitterness, and hatred. Those emotions only compound the tragedy. You are the one who pays the price by carrying the negative emotions with you, allowing them to contaminate every element of your current life. Forgiveness is not a feeling for which you must passively wait to wash over you. Forgiveness is a choice, a choice that you can make to free yourself from the emotional prison of anger, hatred, and bitterness. I am not saying that the "choice" is an easy one, only that it is a necessary one.[7]

Deciding to Forgive

Forgiveness heals and enriches us. In letting go of grievance, anger and resentment, we let go of the tensions and stresses that wound our bodies, poison our minds and our relationships with others and, ultimately, rob us of the possibility of serenity and joy. Forgiving and being forgiven is the "healthy" option. But forgiveness is much, much more than a therapeutic benefit.

In fact, the will to forgive and the decision to forgive, or reject those possibilities is always and profoundly a spiritual decision. It is a decision as to whether we shall live our lives in the world of the constructive word, the creative house of God, or in the desolation and hate of the destructive word.

Forgiveness is not forced on us: it is a choice, a change in our own hearts and reactions, and a gift freely offered to one who does not deserve it. In forgiving, we give up our right to be angry or resentful about an injury unjustly inflicted on us. In making this choice we open our lives to compassion, generosity, and love.[8] From this point of view, forgiveness is a spiritual grace. This is something that all the great religions—Confucian, Hebrew, Christian,

Islamic, Hindu, Sikh, Buddhist, and others—have long understood. The decision to forgive is a commitment to a new way of being.

A Christian View of Forgiveness

Forgiveness is at the very heart of the Christian Gospel. Christ's great message to us is that God has forgiven us for all that we have done wrong. God's forgiveness of us does not *depend* on our willingness to receive it or on our repentance. It is there for all time, manifest through Christ. But until we are willing to acknowledge and accept divine forgiveness, we do not experience it, and we do not respond to it.

Accepting God's forgiveness transforms our lives. We cannot accept this forgiveness and remain unmoved: we begin to live a "forgiven" life, a life filled with the Holy Spirit of God. We cannot accept this forgiven life while remaining ourselves unforgiving. Filled with God's love and with his Spirit, we are moved to offer to others what God has given us: unconditional forgiveness. Forgiveness is the work of the Spirit. Christ's forgiveness comes to us in the Spirit and our forgiveness of others goes to them in the Spirit. Saint Paul says, "If we live by the Spirit, let us also be guided by the Spirit" (Galatians 5:25).

Thus, Jesus tells us to "Love your enemies and pray for those who persecute you" (Matthew 5:44). There is no end to this: we are to forgive "seventy-seven times" (Matthew 18:22). As Gregory Jones says in his excellent study:

> Those who are forgiven by Jesus are called to embody that forgiven-ness in the new life signified by communion with Jesus and with other disciples. Indeed that forgiven-ness calls believers to live penitent lives that seek to reconstruct human relationships in the service of holiness of heart and life.[9]

Forgiveness, therefore, is an important theological concept. It is what God does for us sinners through Christ and what the repentant sinner offers to those who sin against him or her in the power of the Spirit. Jesus said to the disciples, just before he ascended, "Thus it is written, that the Messiah is to suffer and rise from the dead on the third day, and that repentance and forgiveness of sins is to be proclaimed in his name to all nations" (Luke 24:46–47). Forgiveness, God's forgiveness of us, is the gift of salvation.

As Gregory Jones says:

> Christian forgiveness is at once an expression of a commitment to a way of life, the cruciform life of holiness in which we seek to "unlearn" sin and learn the ways of God, and a means of seeking reconciliation in the midst of particular sins, or specific instances of brokenness. In its broadest context, forgiveness is the means by which God's love moves to reconciliation in the face of sin.[10]

Reconsidering the "Unforgivable"

Any discussion of forgiveness will very quickly reveal a great variety of opinions. I have found disagreements even among Christian priests about the nature of forgiveness, or the scope of it. For example, one priest told me that, if someone killed his mother, he would probably be obliged to seek revenge before he could even consider offering forgiveness, for within his culture, this would be demanded of him. Another priest objected very strongly to my teaching that unconditional forgiveness must include everyone, no matter what they have done. He said with great conviction, apropos a world leader: "God may forgive him, but I never will."

Simon Wiesenthal's story of his encounter with an SS officer in a Nazi death camp provides a classic case for a discussion on forgiveness. One day, he was called to a dying SS soldier who wanted to confess his involvement in the murder of Jews and to ask for forgiveness. Wiesenthal listened to the man's appalling confession in silence. When the man asked for his forgiveness so that he could die in peace, Wiesenthal walked away in silence.[11] This is Wiesenthal's own account of this particular encounter. His inability to forgive in this particular case came from his concern that it was not his place to forgive what had been suffered by other people. As far as he as an individual was concerned, he was a man of great forgiving compassion.

What would I have done, in Wiesenthal's place, having lived his life? Are there things that are simply unforgivable?

My Christian conviction is that there is *nothing* that cannot be forgiven. That is, nothing that has been done to myself. I cannot forgive a murderer in the name of the person whom he or she has killed. But I can forgive the perpetrator for the hurt and the loss the murder of a dear one has caused me. There is *nothing* that is so unforgivable that we should nurture hate and grievance, rather than seeking the healing grace of forgiveness. What comes from nurturing such unforgiveness? The consequence is that the wound never heals; hate and bitterness continue generation after generation, poisoning the lives of people not even born when the original crimes were committed. This same sad pattern is obvious in so many places around the world.

Unforgiveness poisons those who do not forgive. It keeps them imprisoned in the hurts and wounds of the past. Forgiveness heals the wounds and liberates the spirit. Forgiveness is a powerful way of healing and liberating the victim. Forgiveness is healing for the forgiver.

Forgiveness is not easy. The worse the injury, the harder it is to forgive. Sometimes we simply cannot forgive, even though we know that as God's forgiven the people, we, too, should forgive. We do not justify inability to forgive, pretending that it is right. Nor do we berate ourselves because we cannot forgive, for we are only human. Rather, we invoke the Spirit to come into our hearts and empower us to forgive. We pray, "Come, Holy Spirit."

Sometimes it can be hard just to open our minds to the possibility of forgiving a terrible offense. We focus on our hurt, on our hate. We do not want to condone terrible actions. We want nothing to do with those who committed them. In fact, we want them punished. All of this seems to us to imply that we cannot forgive, nor even begin the process of forgiveness. But this is a misunderstanding of what forgiveness is—and what it is not.

The Nature of Forgiveness

True forgiveness, which happens in us and to us, is often slow to come and difficult to receive, but it is made more difficult by the many misconceptions that we have of forgiveness. It will therefore be helpful to state clearly what forgiveness is, and what it is not.

Forgiveness is not simply a moral or Christian obligation, imposed from without for the good of those forgiven. Rather, it is our inalienable human right: our inalienable right to let go of pain and grief, to let go of hate and anger, to let go of suffering. We are not obliged to carry those things through the rest of our lives just because someone has injured us! The grace of forgiveness brings healing and wholeness *to those who forgive*. We have an absolute right to that healing. No one should be allowed to rob us of that. If someone has injured us, we have the right not to let that injury poison the rest of our lives.

Forgiveness is not letting the *offender* "off the hook." It lets the *injured person* off the hook of resentment and bitterness. It sets the injured, hurt person free and puts her or him back on the road to wholeness and fulfilled living.

But forgiveness does not mean that we condone the wrong,

nor that we pretend to ourselves that it was not really all that bad. True forgiveness names the wrong, and is clear and honest in declaring it wrong, whereas condoning redefines the wrong and pretends that it was acceptable.

Forgiveness is not excusing the perpetrator of a wrong. Excusing means that the person had an excuse and was therefore excusable. If the person was excusable, there was nothing to forgive. Forgiving is the opposite of excusing. It states clearly that what the person did was wrong and that he or she had no excuse. Indeed the clearest way to say to anyone who has wronged you that he or she is culpable is to say that you forgive them. You are saying, "You had no excuse."

Forgiveness is not tolerating the wrong. On the contrary, forgiveness says in the plainest possible way, "What you did was wrong and hurtful and I will not accept it. I refuse to be your victim."

Forgiveness is not forgetting. "Forgive and forget" is neither a maxim of wisdom nor a goal in life. A wiser maxim is "forgive and remember," but remember in a new way. We cannot forget the hurt, but forgiveness enables us to remember it without resentment and bitterness. Forgiveness enables us to remember in a learning way. We never forget the hurtful experience; we continue to learn from it. I learn about my own vulnerability, my unrealistic expectations, or my proneness to take offense even when no offense was intended.

Forgiveness is not reconciliation. Reconciliation is what happens between you and the person who hurt you. Forgiveness is what happens within you and what you offer to the one who hurt you as your free gift. Forgiveness is not dependent on what is happening between you and the wrongdoer. You can forgive from the heart, even though the person never wants to be reconciled with you. Your forgiveness is never dependent on the other person's willingness to be reconciled. If it were, then the healing of your hurt would then depend on the disposition of another person. Nor does forgiveness require of you a readiness to be reconciled. Jesus said, "Love your enemies." He did not say, "Take them home to tea." An enemy can remain an enemy, even though you have forgiven.

Forgiveness is not a legal pardon. You have every right to demand restitution from the person who wronged you. If necessary, you can bring that person before the courts to receive restitution. When Pope John Paul II went to a prison in Rome and forgave Mehmet Ali Agca for trying to kill him, he was not calling for Agca's release from prison. Agca was accountable for his actions, for which he was paying the price. Accordingly, the Pope was accountable for his response to Agca's action, and so he forgave. There is no inconsistency between the assailant being sentenced to prison and the Pope forgiving the assailant.

Forgiveness is not weakness. It is what a healed person does in strength and power: in the power of the Spirit. Only the healed person can forgive. Forgiveness is saying, "I am now healed of the hurt. I refuse to allow this person to control my life in any way. I offer him or her as a free gift the forgiveness which my healing has made possible." Forgiveness is the strength of Christ forgiving his enemies from the cross.

People who object strongly to the idea that *nothing* is beyond forgiveness, like the priest I mentioned earlier, are really objecting to what forgiveness is not rather than to what forgiveness is. Who can really object to the one thing that liberates the heart and heals the inner wound?

Psychologist Gerald Jampolsky writes:

From the perspective of Love and Spirit, forgiveness is the willingness to let go of the hurtful past. It is the decision to no longer suffer, to heal your heart and soul. It is the choice to no longer find value in hatred or anger. And it is letting go of the desire to hurt others or ourselves because of something that is already in the past. It is willingness to open our eyes to the light in other people rather than to judge or condemn them.[12]

This comprehensive description of forgiveness emphasizes the words *willingness* and *decision*. The same is true of Robert Enright's definition:

Forgiveness is a willingness to abandon one's right to resentment, negative judgment, and indifferent behavior toward one who unjustly injured us, while fostering the undeserved qualities of compassion, generosity, and even love toward him or her.[13]

As psychologists both Enright and Jampolsky focus on the inner states of the mind in the act of forgiving: "willingness to abandon one's right to resentment"; "willingness to let go of the hurtful past"; "decision no longer to suffer"; "choice no longer to find value in hatred or anger"; "letting go of the desire to hurt others"; "willingness to see the light in others"; "willingness to foster love for the one who hurt us." The process of forgiveness begins in us with this desire. It may even be "a desire to desire." A person may be in a situation where he or she is saying, "I wish I could even desire to forgive." Even that "desire for the desire" will open the door to the forgiveness process. That is all the desire the Holy Spirit needs to begin work. The desire is a signal that we want to forgive. We do not want to remain in the prison of hatred or revenge. We recognize that such negative attitudes are bad for our spiritual and physical health. Indeed Dr. Jampolsky writes:

Research into the psychophysiology of human stress has shown us that the thoughts and feelings we hold in our minds are frequently translated into physical symptoms or emotional disorders: anxiety, depression, agitation, poor self-image, headaches, backaches, pains in the neck, stomachaches, and compromised immunity that can make us prone to infection and allergies. It is time to stop attacking our bodies with negative thoughts.[14]

That is why he claims that "forgiveness is the greatest healer of all."

The Desire to Forgive

Where does the desire to forgive come from? Many things can stimulate us to try to forgive one another, or ourselves. Sometimes our motives can be generous or compassionate. Sometimes our motives can be more basic: we want to forgive because we feel that that is what we ought to do, or ought to want in some circumstance. At this level, the desire to forgive develops within the complex thoughts and feelings that comprise our individual psychologies.

Why one first embraces the desire to forgive matters less than whether we truly intend to begin the work of forgiveness. Pretending to forgive, or "going through the motions" without truly letting go of all the anger, hurt, and pain, will do nothing for us. But once we truly want to achieve full forgiveness, all the liberating gifts of healing and integration that forgiveness brings will start to come to us.

The liberation and healing that come from forgiving—and being forgiven—radically alter how we see the people and events that have wounded us, and how we see ourselves. These changes in us are pervasive. They transcend the merely psychological: they bring spiritual growth. For in deciding to forgive, we take charge of our emotions and reactions rather than staying at the mercy of events. This is a giant stride toward a mature responsibility for ourselves and for the meaning of our lives. It is a profound opening up of our spiritual nature. For this reason, Christians have always seen forgiveness both as a powerful tool for developing spiritual strength and as clear evidence of spiritual grace.

The Process of Forgiveness

Getting Ready to Forgive

How does one even start to forgive, especially when a wound is deep? Getting ready to embark on the work of forgiveness is itself a task that may take some time. How can we best do it?

Many people working in this field suggest that there are a number of definite steps one can take, in getting ready to forgive:

- *Reflect.* Think back over what actually happened, what it is that has hurt or angered you. As you do this, try to step back from the situation and see it clearly. Was the hurtful action or word really intended? Was it an uncharacteristic response from a person who was normally friendly? Maybe it was an accident? Or was it a misunderstanding? Before you think of forgiving, you have to be clear about the nature of the hurt, the intention behind the hurt, and the deliberation in causing the hurt. The aim is to understand what it is that you want to forgive.
- *Get in touch with your feelings.* Acknowledge just how recalling this hurt makes you feel: anger, resentment, fury, rage, fear, vengeance, or whatever that feeling may be. The aim here is to understand the burden that you are carrying, because of this wound.

- *Share the understanding you have of both of these things.* Talk to a few close friends about what happened and how you are feeling. Simply sharing these things with another can often bring all the healing you need, or at least bring a fresh perspective to the problem. Many people who believe in God, or a higher power, would choose God, or that higher power, as one of the best friends with whom to share this kind of thought and feeling, sharing their burdens with this higher power and asking for strength, courage, and companionship in the effort to forgive.

Through these steps, we prepare ourselves for forgiveness. But there is more to it than this. The Dalai Lama writes:

A few years back, a Tibetan monk who had served about eighteen years in a Chinese prison in Tibet came to see me after his escape to India. I knew him from my days in Tibet and remembered last seeing him in 1959. During the course of that meeting I had asked him what he felt was the biggest threat or danger while in prison. I was amazed at his answer. It was extraordinary and inspiring. I was expecting him to say something else. Instead, he said that what he most feared was losing his compassion for the Chinese.[15]

Compassion was what he valued most highly in himself. To lose compassion for the Chinese would be a much greater loss than losing his freedom for eighteen years in jail. The loss of compassion would have robbed him of his sense of integrity.

Compassion is the heart of forgiveness. In fully forgiving, we do something far greater than healing our own wounds or making ourselves whole: we are behaving like God, becoming like

God. The enemy may remain hostile, but we are transformed by compassion and love. We are manifesting our capacity for God, our capacity to live in the image of God.

Reframing Our Perspective

A key part of extending compassion to others involves the rediscovery of the humanity of those who have harmed us. Deep hurt may be responsible for our demonizing them, casting them out into outer darkness, expelling them from the face of the earth. We can deny all kinship with them. So long as we dehumanize them in our own minds, we will never move toward healing and forgiveness. The first step into forgiveness is to discover again the kinship of our common humanity. Despite what they have done, they are no less human than we are. We have to change the way we see them. This is called "reframing."

Joanna North writes:

> Enright and his colleagues have described reframing as a process whereby the wrongdoer is viewed in context in an attempt to build up a complete picture of the wrongdoer and his actions. Typically, this involves understanding the pressures that the wrongdoer was under at the time of the wrong and an appreciation of the wrongdoer's personality as a result of his particular developmental history.[16]

Reframing helps us to separate the wrongdoer from the wrong he or she has committed. When someone does something bad, it is a natural instinct to see only the bad and to see the person as a "bad person." But there is more to the person than the "bad" that he or she has done. We should not confuse the sinner with the sin; we should not identify the wrongdoer with the wrong.

We should separate the person from the evil he or she does. The Christian maxim is that we hate the sin but not the sinner. We condemn the wrong but forgive the wrongdoer.

Gaining Control Over Our Feelings

Forgiveness involves letting go of violent emotions, such as hate. For example, to help people whose loved ones have been murdered, Luskin uses a technique he calls PERT: Positive Emotional Refocusing Technique. He has used the PERT technique with groups of women from Northern Ireland, both Catholic and Protestant, who saw their sons or husbands killed in the troubles. And, in follow-up studies, he discovered that the forgiveness that they arrived at by using this technique remained with them.

The technique consists of four very simple psychological practices:

- Bring your attention fully to your stomach as you draw in two or three deep breaths. On the in-breath feel the stomach gently expand. On the out-breath feel the stomach gently soften and relax.
- On the third breath bring your mind's eye to some beautiful scene that fills you with awe and delight. A scene from nature, like the Grand Canyon, or from art, like the Sistine Chapel.
- While visualizing, breathe deeply into your stomach.
- Ask the relaxed part of you what you can do to resolve the difficulty.

This bodily and psychological technique is good preparation for coming to terms with any problem. It is much like our centering prayer, in many ways. Like that prayer, it will induce stillness and calm, and every problem is easier to handle in that mental state than when we are agitated. Through the chapters of this book, we have taken this a step further: we have added the extra dimension of preparing ourselves for life by filling ourselves with love, with self-acceptance, and with gratitude and joy for good things. It is important to take that extra step, when faced with the challenges of forgiving. In tackling things that are wounding or distressing in life, it is important not to lose sight of the positive, healing things: friends, beautiful things and places, good times, the strengths, skills, and virtues that we ourselves have.

I have to gain control over how I think and feel if I am to forgive. If I am not in control of my inner self, if my thoughts are in turmoil and my emotions are boiling over in each new crisis, I am not in a fit state to make a reasonable response in any situation of conflict. My difficulty in forgiving in a particular situation may be pointing to a deeper problem in my life: I may be living in such a way that my thoughts and emotions are completely undisciplined, swayed by every new provocation. This is no basis for inner strength. Practicing the skills of becoming calm, of self-control, and of forgiveness will introduce me to a deeper interior life.

Helping Others to Forgive?

Forgiveness is a profound grace, a gift that we can achieve through spiritual strength, through inner strength. Does this mean that we are powerless to help others toward the healing grace of forgiveness? No!

We can help one another to forgive and heal. But in this we must be patient, sensitive, and compassionately oriented to the other. We try first to discern the hurt person's current state—or stage—of grievance. Then, we accept that stage and honor how the person is feeling in that stage. But accepting and honoring does not mean that we do not challenge the person to move forward.

We may have to say, "I know you feel very much the victim right now but you will not remain a victim for the rest of your life. God will heal you and you will forgive." By staying patiently beside hurting people, helping them to recognize where they are hurting, keeping them open to the great mystery of God's forgiving love poured into their hearts, we can gently lead them along the path of forgiveness. Then one day they will wake up and discover that they have forgiven.

Forgiving Myself

Have you ever said to yourself, *I will never forgive myself*? Sadly, people not only say that, but they also mean it. We can hold "vengeance against ourselves." We have failed in some serious way; we are hurting on the inside. Instead of accepting the fact of the weakness that led to our failure, we punish and denounce ourselves as stupid, or awful, or no good. We resent not so much the fact of failure, but ourselves for having failed. We nourish a grievance against ourselves. We refuse to accept ourselves.

Carl Jung described the dynamic of refusing to forgive oneself in this way:

> The acceptance of oneself is the essence of the moral problem and the epitome of a whole outlook on life. That I feed the hungry, that I forgive an insult, and that I love my enemy as myself in the name of Christ are all undoubtedly great virtues. What I do unto the least of my brethren, that I do unto Christ. But what if I should discover that the least amongst them all, the poorest of the beggars, the most impudent of all the offenders, the very enemy himself—these are within me, and that I myself stand in need of the arms of my own kindness. What if I am the enemy to be loved, what then? As a rule the Christian

attitude is then reversed. There is no longer any question of love or long suffering. We condemn and rage against ourselves, we hide from the world, and we refuse to admit ever having met this least lowly in ourselves. Had it been Christ himself who drew near to us in this despicable form, we should have denied him a thousand times before a single cock had crowed.[17]

We can and should extend to ourselves the very same forgiveness that we receive, or the very same forgiveness that we want to offer to others. In fact, if we do not forgive ourselves, or if we remain angry with and rejecting of ourselves, we are in no position to accept the forgiveness that others may offer us. We are also unable to offer forgiveness to anyone else. Therefore, we are not in the right spiritual state to forgive or to be forgiven.

How is one to forgive oneself? When we harbor anger and grievance against ourselves, we are "a house divided." Both the individual who failed and the individual who is ashamed or hurt by that failure live in the same skin. In fact, "they" are one and the same person. Fully accepting that fact is the only way to forge a reconciliation with yourself. This act of acceptance is more subtle and may have more far-reaching effects than we suppose. For in accepting that *both* the inadequate side of myself *and* the side of myself that deserves better are *one and the same*, I am accepting, first, that I am not perfect and, second, that even the imperfect in me deserves to be treated well and loved. This more unified view of myself can free me to love myself in my entirety, even though I have messed some things up. It opens the door to forgiving myself in a profound and enriching way. It is in this spirit that Christians may thank God for all that they are, confidently placing themselves, in their entirety, warts and all, in God's hands.

Exercise

Center yourself, using the techniques we learned in chapter one.

- Bring yourself to stillness and calm.
- Feel yourself enfolded in love, as before.
- Open your mind to how you feel about yourself. Are you harboring resentments against yourself? Are there things for which you have not forgiven yourself?
- Examine the memories and the feelings that come as you do this. Perhaps it helps to focus on one particular thing. Experience your thoughts and feelings, and then gently let them go. Forgive yourself, as much as you can today.
- Now focus on your breathing again. Bring yourself back to stillness, calm.
- Turn your mind now to all the good that is in you, and rejoice as you learned to do in the exercise at the end of chapter five. Bring yourself back to stillness and calm, and then gently back to the world.

Forgiving is a central theme in Christ's teaching. The technique for forgiving ourselves described here is very much like a strong Christian practice, where, at the start of our eucharistic services, we call to mind our faults and failings in a moment of regret, and then leave them behind. We forgive ourselves, and this self-forgiveness is reinforced by the words of the priest, who reminds us that we have also been forgiven by God. We are now free to open ourselves to spiritual growth.

7

Fulfilling Our Potential

Ransomed, healed, restored, forgiven.

H. F. LYTE

If you have worked through this book with me, you will already have made a very profound inner journey. Through the cumulative practice of our centering prayer, you will have learned to still and calm your body; to feel loved, and therefore lovable; to "lighten up" in the judgments you make of yourself, the attitudes you hold to yourself. You will have learned to rejoice in the good within and around you, even if you, or your world, are far from perfect. You will have learned to forgive yourself.

This inner journey is powerfully healing, at many levels. As we saw at the start of this book, meditative practices of the kind we have followed through each successive chapter are good for the body. It is good to be able to relax our bodies, let go of tension and agitation and be still and calm. The meditative activities we have used are also healing for the mind and heart. Which of us does not feel safer, more comfortable, and happier when we feel loved and lovable? Who is not restored and soothed by moving toward a proper balance between his or her flaws and virtues, a balance that accepts that we are not perfect, *and do not need to be*, to be a lovable and valuable human being? Forgiving yourself, accepting yourself in these ways, brings not only physical calm but also psychological calm, and even joy. It is healing for the mind, as well as the body. Perhaps even more important than gains at either of these levels is the fact that these meditative practices that we have learned are also healing for the spirit. They take us far beyond the physical calm that restores our material self, the self composed of flesh, blood, muscle, nerve, and bone. They take us far beyond the psychological calm that comes from getting our traits, our characters, and our behavior in perspective, and from letting go of destructive emotions and thoughts. These practices take us to the very heart of spirituality, and to the spiritual calm that comes from loving and valuing yourself as the unique individual that you are; an individual with a unique place in the complex fabric of existence; an individual so securely rooted in that sense of being valuable that you can rise above the setbacks and wounds of everyday life, and take responsibility for how you respond, rather than being passively blown about by events.

Calming the body is not so very hard. Sometimes, it can seem all but impossible, as we struggle with problems and pressures, snowed under by anxiety or consumed with rage. Psychological healing, coming to feel safe, acceptable and adequate, is much harder still. For most of us, it is a daily struggle, something we must work for over and over again, as we try to cope with the unpredictability of life, losses and griefs, criticisms and rejections from others, and our failure to live up to our own standards, to meet the goals we have set ourselves, or to realize our dreams. Spiritual maturity is the hardest to achieve of all. It requires us to look beyond the immediate world we inhabit, to step back, as it were, and to begin living by values that transcend our automatic reactions to the ups and downs of the material world. Spiritual maturity requires us to center our sense of value on what is eternal, rather than what is immediate and ephemeral.

Rudyard Kipling captured something of what this means, in one of his best-loved poems with these most famous lines:

> If you can meet with triumph and disaster
> And treat those two imposters just the same....[1]

Perhaps the great popularity of this poem comes from its succinct expression of something we all feel, and long for: the spiritual strength to *cope*, to *remain ourselves*, *the very best selves we can be* whatever life may throw at us. This kind of inner strength and inner conviction that we matter *separately* from the details of our histories or our circumstances is what we are striving for when we search for spirituality. And it is obvious, from this, that we cannot have a powerful spirituality without good self-esteem.

The Conviction That We Matter

Where does it come from, this spiritual conviction that we matter in a profound way that transcends our human histories or circumstances? Where does the spiritual strength to treat triumph and disaster "just the same" come from?

For those who believe in a benevolent higher power or Creator, this conviction is underwritten by faith in the idea that our "eternal" significance, and the eternal significance of our values, come from that Power. For me as a Catholic, all human life is necessarily precious, because it is precious to God. This is wonderfully reassuring. It is the firm foundation of my spiritual strength. But many people either cannot make that leap of faith at all or waver in their conviction.

I told a story, earlier, of a man who falls down a cliff, catches a shrub to stop his fall and calls for help. God responds, but despite the man's protests that he believes that God can save him and will do whatever God asks of him, the man cannot obey when God tells him to let go of the shrub. Such moments of doubt, of wavering belief, must be familiar to virtually everyone who believes in God, or in any higher power! But at least individuals in this position are, at some level, accepting of the idea of their own existence in relation to an entity that transcends the material world and gives them significance and value. Such people have a basis to work from, in developing an ever stronger faith in their own eternal, transcendental, spiritual significance.

But what of people who have no faith in any higher power or God? Where can spiritual strength come from for such people? Their position is more as if, after falling off the cliff, they had not themselves heard the voice of God, but someone on the beach below had shouted up, "God's there for you! He'll save you if you let go of the shrub!" This is an altogether greater leap of faith than that asked of the man in the original story. It looks very much like a leap too far.

Christ's invitation is to all of us. He is like the person at the bottom of the cliff who can see God directly, where we may not, as we dangle from the frail shrub. The invitation is to believe that we *are* all uniquely and eternally significant, valuable, and loved because we are the children of God. It is an invitation to believe that we *are* capable of godlike behavior that transcends the vicissitudes of material life. We are not invited to let go of a mere shrub, but of the things that hold us back from our spiritual development, and from fulfilling our full potential as beings who *need not* be limited and defined by the things that happen to us, or by the things we possess or do not possess, or by the value others place on us. We are not invited to let go of a lifeline, but, rather, to have faith in *ourselves*, to value *ourselves* for the rich potential that is within us. And whether you can, at the moment, accept the help of a higher power or not, accepting *that* invitation is the doorway to developing spiritual strength.

Spiritual Development

The exercises at the end of each chapter of this book are tools that can be used to help spiritual development. Each one centers the self in stillness and quiet, and brings thoughts, feelings, and events into perspective. Such practices are tools for working toward that kind of detachment that is not the slave to "knee-jerk" responses, whether in triumph or disaster. But what, eventually, might be the fruits of embarking on this task? What sorts of change come about, through continuously building up your spiritual strength?

Often, we hear the fruits of spiritual development spoken of as "gains in enlightenment," or "conversions." But what, exactly, are these things? How do they come about?

Sometimes we hear of people who have suffered very sudden conversions, as if they had been struck by one blinding flash of insight that forever changes the way they see things and the way they live. Such things happen, on a greater or lesser scale, to most of us, in some area of life, or at some moment. But, for the most part, spiritual development is not a matter of one sudden transformation in the way we are. Rather, it is a gradual and slow process, a process that requires a great deal of work, of reflection and openness to change. It is a process that takes time, effort, persistence, and patience.

But what is involved in this spiritual development or conversion? What, exactly, is the work we must do to achieve it? Donald Gelpi, a Jesuit theologian, defines conversion in this way: "It is the decision to reject irresponsible choices and to assume responsibility for one's subsequent development in some area of human experience."[2]

Conversion starts from the recognition that I am not living fully the life that God gives me. I am not fully inhabiting my life, not fully experiencing or valuing the unique entity that is me. I am not using the gift of life as fully as I could. Much of the work we have done through the exercises at the end of successive chapters in this book is the work we need to do to start putting that right: coming to know ourselves fully as forgiven, acceptable, and loved.

But just as the realization that I am loved and forgiven releases a peace and joy that overflow so that I am moved to offer that love and forgiveness to others, so the acceptance that my worth lies in the realms of love and forgiveness changes my fundamental values and my orientation to life.

Self-esteem reflects the values we apply in judging ourselves. When those values are unrealistic or wrong, when they set false standards—standards that we cannot meet so that we feel bad and deny our worth—we may feel like failures and treat ourselves badly. Finding better values that are rooted in the spiritual not the material, and in faithfulness not success, sets us free to love and accept ourselves, and so to treat ourselves well. And as we treat ourselves, so we will tend to treat others. "Love your neighbor as you love yourself" is not only a pious hope, as we might take it to be; it is also a description of what we tend to do. If I only love myself when I am rich and famous, I will not love you if you are poor and voiceless.

The question that follows from establishing a strong spiritual basis for my own self-esteem is, *Where do I go from here?* And the answer is that I must develop the spiritual values that sustain my own self-esteem and extend those values to others. Achieving my true potential becomes a matter of growing in love, in kindness, in mercy, and in justice.

Spiritual Fulfillment
and Social Justice

Fulfillment can be a purely individual thing. I can choose to live a rich inner life, valuing myself without reflecting on the plight of others, and without taking any responsibility for the social or economic or political order under which I and others have to live. I can ignore the basic law of my humanity: that all human existence has to be coexistence.

Many Christians, for example, lived happily in South Africa under apartheid, without feeling any need to challenge the way in which black South Africans were totally excluded and marginalized in their own country. For centuries, Christian Europe and America lived with slavery. Many of us today live with and vote for socioeconomic systems that are radically inequitable, where the few are wealthy and the majority poor. Many Christians today accept practices that favor rich nations at the expense of the poor, or that favor the better off in our own communities at the expense of those at the margins of society, such as the poor, the ill-educated, those with disabilities, and immigrants. For many Christians, religious and moral values have to do with individual life and behavior, and have nothing to do with politics or how society is organized and functions. These Christians have "privatized" their faith and morality, restricting it to the privacy of their own souls. While they seek the good for their own life, they do not feel impelled to seek the common good, or to work for the betterment of the disadvantaged of society.

Pope John Paul II criticizes this approach to spirituality as stunted when he speaks about the need for a broader view of what it means to live out our full potential in relation to spiritual values. He speaks of the need for "solidarity." We are all interdependent. My very independence can only be guaranteed by a constructive interdependence. We need one another for our very survival. Pope John Paul II wrote in his encyclical "On Social Concerns":

> When interdependence becomes recognized in this way, the correlative response as a moral and social attitude, or a "virtue," is solidarity. This is not a feeling of vague compassion or shallow distress at the misfortunes of so many people both near and far. On the contrary, it is a firm and persevering determination to commit oneself to the common good; that is to say, to the good of all and of each individual because we are all really responsible for all.[3]

Pope John Paul II argues that achieving our full spiritual potential must involve a change of heart or a "conversion" that extends our values to others through this commitment to solidarity, a virtue which enables us to challenge what he calls the "social structures of sin." When we as a nation or as a Church or community encounter "structures of sin" and oppression, institutionalized racism, or sectarianism, we have to challenge those structures. We are called to a sociopolitical conversion, to assume responsibility for the common good. Sociopolitical conversion will mean that we will seek to change oppressive social or political structures and we will get involved in the politics of change, either on the local or the national level. And if we find these structures of oppression and exclusion within the framework of our own Church, within the texture of our own religious culture or society, solidarity with the oppressed will make us challenge those structures all the more persistently. Living the virtue of solidarity ensures that I will never live a life isolated from the concerns of this world, thinking only of myself. As John Paul II says, "We must reject the temptation to offer a privatized and individualistic spirituality which ill accords with the demands of charity."[4]

True spirituality cannot flourish or realize its full potential in the isolated self. If only I exist, if only I have spiritual significance, then all the others that I interact with, all the things I do, must be meaningless. But the others I interact with, the things I do, form the physical and psychological foundations of my being. If these become meaningless, my very existence is fragmented and devalued—the very opposite of what is involved in spiritual strength. For this reason, spirituality can only flourish if it extends beyond the self, to embrace others. If *I* matter, and am of significance, and I use my time and gifts interacting in important ways with *you*, then *you, too,* must matter and be significant. You, too, must deserve love and respect, just as I do. It is seeing this that makes us spiritually whole.

In the words of John Paul II:

> A spirituality of communion implies also the ability to see what is positive in others, to welcome it and to prize it as a gift from God: not only as a gift for the brother or sister who has received it directly, but also as a "gift for me." A spirituality of communion means, finally, to know how to "make room" for our brothers and sisters, bearing "each other's burdens" (Galatians 6:2) and resisting the selfish temptations which constantly beset us and provoke competition, careerism, distrust and jealousy.[5]

It is tempting to interpret this kind of exhortation to social solidarity as an exhortation to involve ourselves in the "big" issues of social justice: the political campaigns for equality and justice and the charities that feed the victims of famine and war, and the like. And indeed, we must realize that all the beneficiaries of such campaigns are individuals like ourselves, and they are as valuable and special as we are because of their individuality. But engaging social solidarity only at this level holds others at arm's length. We, and the beneficiaries of our compassion, remain anonymous and unknown to one another. True spiritual strength demands that we go further than this. It demands that we actively extend love and respect to others in a very personal way, in a way that embraces and responds to their individual identity. Of course, we cannot do that for the millions who are hungry, or for the millions who are oppressed. But we can do it for the particular individuals who cross our paths each day: for fellow travelers in the train to work, for the worker at the checkout in the supermarket, for those we work with, for our friends, and for our families.

Realizing our full potential in these ways is hard. It involves a change of heart at many levels. It is not enough simply to develop our own spirituality and our own understanding and acceptance of ourselves. It is not enough simply to forgive others for the wrongs they have done us. We have to start all over again and question how we relate to others; that is, how we *should* relate to others. This involves changes in our emotional responses, our intellectual understanding and our moral values. It needs growth and development at all of these levels.

Emotional Development

Emotional development means taking responsibility for all of my emotions, all my feelings. It can be rightly called "emotional conversion." I must learn not to repress or deny my feelings, even my very negative feelings, but to recognize each one and acknowledge it.

This process involves reexamining our feelings about other people, as well as our feelings about ourselves. What, truthfully, do we *honestly* feel about people of other backgrounds, genders, age-groups, religions, classes, colors, nationalities, or sexual and political orientations, for example? Only when we acknowledge such feelings truthfully can we bring our reactions under scrutiny and begin to examine how legitimate they really are, or how prejudiced we are, or how well our feelings match up to our spiritual values. We know we were not born with these feelings. None of us was born with a racial prejudice, for example, yet anyone of us can become racially prejudiced. Why is that?

We all know people who are quite religious, and, yet, full of prejudice, whether the prejudice is racial or religious in origin. This is not spiritual fulfillment. If I feel negative or bad about other races, particularly the new immigrant and refugee groups, I have to ask myself, *Where does this feeling come from and how am I integrating this feeling into my life of faith?* Emotional development helps us to deal initially with repressed negative emotions. We assume responsibility for hidden motivations in our actions and we seek not to be controlled or enslaved by our repressed anger, guilt, fear, or whatever.[6] Sectarianism, racism, sexism, color prejudice, and the like breed in emotional hurts. Emotional conversion opens the way for these hurts to be healed. A person who has truly espoused spiritual values of love, acceptance, and forgiveness will not be going around with a chip on his or her shoulder about other races, religions or traditions, and so on. He or she will truly respect others, whoever they may be. As Saint Paul put it, after his famous and dramatic conversion to Christianity on the road to Damascus: "There is no longer Jew or Greek, there is no longer slave or free…for all of you are one in Christ Jesus" (Galatians 3:28).

It is possible to be full of spiritual thoughts but still harbor many hostile, negative feelings. Fulfilling your potential means growing beyond this stage. It means reviewing your emotional reactions in the light of your spiritual values, and bringing the two into harmony. This process takes time and effort, sometimes struggle. But achieving a proper harmony here takes us to a higher plane. It liberates the mind and broadens horizons. Emotional development or conversion opens up the possibility of relating to others in a new way.

Intellectual Development

In the pursuit of emotional development, we inevitably find ourselves confronting beliefs that sustain our feelings: *immigrants steal our jobs*, for example, or *women are not so reliable as men in a workforce*. Intellectual development is the process through which we examine and explore these beliefs and challenge their truth or falsity. It is the process through which we take responsibility for what we believe, and for the adequacy or otherwise of the knowledge on which those beliefs are based. It is a true conversion of thinking.

Intellectual development is a matter of embracing intellectual honesty, and of rooting one's judgments in knowledge that is *not* based upon preconception or prejudice. For example, people who have never read anything about Islam or other religions should not be pontificating about those religions anymore than those who know nothing of my own faith should be making accusations against it. Sometimes Catholics are accused of "worshipping" our Lady, or of being set free to sin by being pardoned through the sacrament of reconciliation and let loose to do it all again next week. Those who make such outlandish claims often refuse to read anything the Catholic Church actually teaches on Catholic devotion to the Mother of God or to make the slightest enquiry as to what is actually involved in reconciliation. I may see this prejudice against my faith for the intellectual dishonesty that it is, but yet fail to notice other intellectual dishonesty of my own. Intellectual honesty can only be maintained by a willingness to undergo an intellectual conversion in each new situation.

Intellectual development brings with it a humility of mind and enables the person to live with uncertainty and with the realization that he or she might be wrong. Intellectual development will always enhance one's self-esteem. Seeking to understand, refusing to pass judgments in ignorance, keeping one's mind open, these are the signs of good self-esteem.

Equally, intellectual development will open our mind to other ideas in a new way. When we enter a dialogue with others who have very different views and beliefs from our own, we should be open to listening to their ideas, open to explaining our own, with no prior agenda of imposing our own beliefs on the other. We should invite all to participate in dialogue as a free and full expression of identity. Our aim is understanding, not control: understanding what they believe and why they believe it. Too often, "dialogue" between those of different beliefs, whether those beliefs are political, religious, or scientific, can be a dialogue of the deaf. Too often, rules are drawn up that prevent a true dialogue from ever developing. If I refuse to listen to some idea of yours, how can I come to know what you believe, or why? And if I do not know these things, how can I be intellectually honest in my reflections on your beliefs? Being ignorant of what someone else believes is not dishonest; passing judgments based on that ignorance is.

Moral Development

As we relate to people more openly and honestly, through emotional development, and as we understand and evaluate beliefs more honestly through intellectual development or conversion, we will come inevitably to reconsider the detail of our moral code.

Morality is about the good, the right thing to do. Our understanding of just what that is changes as our knowledge of ourselves and of other people grows. The psychologist Lawrence Kohlberg identified three main phases of this development, as we pass from infancy to adult life: first, the *preconventional* phase, in which "good" means no more than what we are praised for by others, or what gives us personal satisfaction, and "bad" is what we are punished for, or what makes us personally dissatisfied. (The *preconventional* stage is concerned solely with the child's own needs without reference to others.) Second, there is the *conventional* stage, in which "good" means what supports social relationships, either between individuals or in society at large, and "bad" means things that disrupt social interactions at any level. (The *conventional* stage is concerned with the expectations of society and society's laws, the "conventions of society.") Third, there is the *postconventional* stage, at which good and bad are defined in terms of values that transcend any particular social relationship or society, any particular individual or circumstance: values that are rooted in human universals.[7] (The *postconventional* stage is concerned with more personal principles that are not necessarily defined by society's laws or the conventions of one's society.) These turn out, inevitably, to be spiritual values, such as the right to life, the right to dignity and respect; the right, for example, for each and every one of us to be valued, just as we are.

Kohlberg's three stages of moral development can capture moral beliefs across all the cultures in which researchers have explored them. Carol Gilligan, a collaborator with Kohlberg, went on to criticize his research on the grounds that it was too male-dominated, and that it did not reflect female psychological and moral development.[8] At the earliest stage, there is great difference between individuals in just what is seen as good or bad, reflecting the tastes and circumstances of different individuals. Nonetheless, the *principle* on which these judgments rest is always the same: for the *preconventional*, "morality" is a matter of punishment or praise, satisfaction or dissatisfaction. At the *conventional* stage, too, there are great differences between cultures in just what is seen as being for the good of the social system or for the good of individual relationships—for example, note the vast differences between Capitalism and Communism, yet each was formulated as a system for the good of society. Nonetheless, the principle on which moral decisions are made is always in terms of how particular actions support or undermine social relations. Within a single culture, opinions on what is good or bad begin to become less varied, as they come to reflect the status quo in that society. At the *postconventional* stage, moral decisions become remarkably more similar across individuals and cultures. This is inevitable, because morality is defined in terms of human universals at this stage of development.

The *preconventional* stage is the stage of childhood. The satisfaction of need and the avoidance of punishment or disapproval by others are the guiding norms. The child does not take into account the conventions of his or her society. Yet many adults remain fixed at this stage, at least in some areas of their moral thinking: for we are not consistent in how we approach moral dilemmas, moving between one approach and another. The *conventional* stage is typical of adult life, the main way of thinking of the average adult. If it is lawful it must be good, if it is unlawful it must be bad. Conform to the conventions of one's society and you will be a respectable citizen. Only a minority of individuals reach the *postconventional* stage of moral development. Yet all of us have the means of reaching for this postconventional approach: all of us have the potential for rooting our morality in spiritual values, and for doing what is right simply because it is right.

The great Jesuit philosopher Bernard Lonergan wrote: "Moral conversion [that is, development] changes the criterion of one's decisions and choices from satisfactions to values."[9] According to Kohlberg, this is a call to develop our morality from a preconventional to a postconventional basis. Where there is a clash between my personal satisfaction or comfort, and doing what is universally right, which do I choose? Too often we make the wrong choice. How many people place the satisfaction of proving themselves right, before the peace and tranquillity of other relationships, for example? And how many good relationships ultimately break up because one partner always places the satisfaction of getting his or her own way before everything else? Choosing moral values over personal satisfaction can sometimes be difficult. Do I, for example, stop to help when I am first on the scene of a car crash, even though I am late, it is raining hard, and who knows what blood, horror, and risk of being injured I will face? Intuitively, we know what we *should* do, or what is morally correct in such a situation. Full moral development means not only acknowledging that spiritual values such as the right to life, respect, and dignity must always take precedence over the comfort and satisfaction of the individual, but also committing ourselves to living out that moral conviction.

Adopting the universal spiritual values of the *postconventional* stage brings meaning and direction to our morality and to our lives. Universal truths are "just what it says on the packet": universally true. There is no randomness in these truths, they do not change by the vicissitudes of public opinion or political change. They remain, as always, the same. In adopting these spiritual values as my basis for moral judgment, my basis for action, I fully realize my potential and my value as a human being.

Choosing to Grow

As my development in any one area progresses, it will open up new questions in other areas. Moral understanding, intellectual understanding, and emotional understanding all interrelate, feeding back to one another to create an ever more integrated whole. Development is never an all-or-nothing thing, it is never over in a flash. In this most central area of our lives, development will never end as we seek deeper and deeper understanding of ourselves, of our values, and of other people.

It is up to each of us to choose how we will live our lives, how far we will strive for moral, emotional, and intellectual development, and for the spiritual development that this inevitably implies. No one can compel us to develop or to grow into our full potential as a human beings. We can choose, instead, to remain nothing more than a collection of material possessions and other people's opinions of our reputation. Or we can choose to strive for spiritual development and fulfillment through the spiritual. We can, in other words, decide to follow our own conscience and not be swayed by the expectations of our society or our friends. I can only realize my full, human potential when I faithfully act according to my conscience. I know in my heart what I should do and what I should not do. When I am genuinely confused about what is right and what is wrong I know I have to resolve my dilemmas in accordance with my deepest convictions. Deciding to live faithfully according to my conscience each day calls for my daily conversion on some level if not all of the levels we have just discussed.

Spirituality and Religion

Through spiritual development, we can opt for a way of life that is a faithful embodiment of our sense of self-worth. If we believe that we are precious in God's sight, if we believe that we are persons of great intrinsic worth, we will give expression to these deep-core beliefs in the way we live and act. We speak about making our fundamental option for the good. That is, to opt for the good over the bad, the true over the false, love over hatred, kindness over meanness. In making our fundamental option for the good, we take responsibility for our lives, and we give meaning and direction to our lives.

Many of us yearn for spiritual development: to understand ourselves, and to shape our lives in terms of spiritual values rather than material ones. We instinctively understand that we are more than our possessions, more than our public reputations. We long for spiritual understanding—but baulk at conventional religion as a way to find it.

"Belief in God" does not necessarily involve any kind of religious commitment. In fact, the sociologist Grace Davie says that there is a phenomenon of "believing without belonging." The vast majority of people believe in God, but do not belong to any church. She argues that most people are just as religious, in their own way, as other people, but that they practice a form of "vicarious" religion. That is, they are happy that the churches are there, and that some people attend them, because one day they themselves might need them.[10]

Being religious does not necessarily mean that one has yet achieved much spiritual development. Even externally devout and religious people often maintain an unconverted heart, a heart that has not yet opened itself to universal truths and values. Belonging to a religion is no guarantee of development. Yet, the great religions offer us support in this journey, if we are prepared to commit ourselves.

Pope Paul VI described the Christian conversion that leads to life like this: "We can only approach the Kingdom of Christ by *metanoia*. This is a profound change of the whole person by which we begin to consider, judge, and arrange our life according to the holiness and love of God."[11] To consider, judge, and arrange our life according to the love of God calls for that fundamental shift, that radical option for value over satisfaction. It is this that comes through in every aspect of Jesus' teaching. Nothing can enhance our lives more than following this advice.

Gelpi writes:

By religious conversion I mean the decision to respond responsibly to the free, gratuitous, historical self-disclosure and self-communication of God. By Christian conversion I mean the decision to respond responsibly to the definitive, free, gratuitous, historical self-disclosure and self-communication of God accomplished in Jesus and in the illuminating power of the Breath that proceeds him.[12]

Religious conversion is always a response to a gift. It cannot take place naturally. It is a response in faith. True religious conversion is a personal response to an invitation from God to enter into a loving, trusting relationship. We cannot give ourselves religious faith. Only God can give us faith. And, even with this faith that God gives, the believer has to pray, "I believe; help my unbelief!" (Mark 9:24).

The Challenge of Spirituality

To be human is to develop. We are built with the capacity for emotional, intellectual, and moral development. The psychological processes that serve these forms of development are the tools that lead us, inevitably, to spiritual values. As the great theologians of the Middle Ages would say, "Grace builds on nature." Grace presupposes the natural. It builds on and perfects the natural. The development that realizes our full potential will always have a spiritual dimension of grace.

The highest spiritual values are universal, transcending time and place, and transcending the particulars of our histories and circumstances. They give us a powerful basis for esteeming ourselves, and for relating to others in constructive and life-giving ways. We are all valuable, and we all have the right to life, to respect, and to dignity. How much human pain and suffering would be avoided, if only we could all live out those values?

My conviction is that the spiritual values that open our lives to fulfillment, to peace and joy, and to a sense of our own absolute worth come from the higher power that I call God.

There is no area in my life, once I hand it over to God (or to my higher power), in which I cannot grow, or in which I cannot come into true freedom. The grace of conversion is God's way of dealing with all my refusal to grow, my unwillingness to take responsibility, and my settling for a way of life that would not reflect the person I truly am. My way of life should be the embodiment of those basic truths about myself: a person who is precious in God's sight, a person who is lovable, a person who has the capacity for God and, therefore, a person who is loving, kind and forgiving. That is the kind of person each of us is invited to be. Our response to this invitation is entirely within our own power.

Exercise

Center yourself, using the techniques we learned in chapter one.

- Bring yourself to stillness and calm.
- Feel yourself enfolded in love, as before.
- Open your mind to what you have read in this book and to how you have reacted to what you have read. Notice the thoughts you have, the feelings.
- Now ask yourself: *How committed am I to finding real spiritual strength and to bringing my spirituality to the highest level I can? How much effort am I prepared to put into achieving spiritual development right now?*
- Now focus on your breathing again. Bring yourself back to stillness, calm, and then gently back to the world.

This question of how much we want spiritual strength, how much we are prepared to do to achieve it, is the core question for anyone of us. It is the core question for a Christian. *Would I rather just get on with the immediate tasks, the immediate events in front of me, making the most of the material world? Or do the values that transcend the material matter enough to me to give them precedence?*

Epilogue

*"My grace is sufficient for you; for power
is made perfect in weakness."*

2 CORINTHIANS 12:9

A waterfall is a stunning sight. Above the fall, the river is beautiful and tranquil, passing through lands mysterious and attractive. Below, beyond the fall, it is the same: peaceful, full of the promise that the life-giving water brings. But in the fall itself, there is such power, such turmoil, an overwhelming force that carries everything before it, that blocks out everything around it, as if nothing exists but the fall.

There is something utterly arresting about a waterfall. I have watched men and women gaze in wonder at the beauty of Niagara Falls in Canada, and stand speechless before the majestic splendor of the Victoria Falls in Africa. I have traveled with members of my family a full day over rugged terrain to catch a glimpse of Angel Falls in Venezuela. Tired and exhausted, we sat and watched the translucent water as it cascaded down the fall. Confronted by such a sight, we are reminded of the great forces of life that surround us, the power and the glory of such forces, and our human weakness in comparison.

Each human life has its waterfall moments. We float along on the safe, calm river of our lives, and then, maybe without warning, or maybe having heard the distant thunder of the approaching fall, we round a bend and are suddenly thrown out of our tranquillity, wrenched from our comfort zone; helplessly swept over the brink into a terrifying maelstrom that takes all our resources simply to survive.

Perhaps we experience such struggles as adventure: the ecstasy of the adrenalin rush of white-water rafting taken to the extreme. Perhaps we experience these struggles as sheer horror, an unwelcome destruction of the life we loved, or would have liked to keep. I hope this book has encouraged you toward the idea that we have a choice in how we react to such events. What can seem like a disaster, misery, horror, destruction, and failure may turn out to be no less than the passage from one part of the river of life to another. Instead of terrorizing us, the "waterfalls" on our river of life can be moments of ecstasy, moments that remind us that we are in fact alive, with all the highs and lows, the confusions and uncertainties, that life entails. The choice is ours; and the choice is a spiritual one: *How will I respond to this challenge? How will I value myself through it?* And it is this spiritual choice that is at the heart of true self-esteem.

The psalmist says of humanity that God has "crowned them with glory and honor" (Psalm 8:5). Nowhere in life are that glory and honor so obvious as in our waterfall moments, as life becomes disrupted, fractured, and we find ourselves in free fall. We may feel out of control, helplessly carried along by events—good or bad—but our old tranquillity is disrupted, either way. We are brought alive.

To see such challenges as opportunities for growth is itself an act of faith: faith in yourself, whatever the outcome. And actually, all of us, without exception, deserve that faith! How arrogant, how deluded we would think a log if it blamed *itself* for Niagara Falls. If nothing else, I hope that this book has encouraged you to see that you are valuable, you are of infinite value, no matter how turbulent and challenging the waters of your life may be. Once we reflect on the beauty of our human life, as we have done in this book, we become aware of our dignity, our self-worth, and our value. We get in touch again with our experience of love and freedom. We remember with gratitude our ecstasy of joy and freedom. We view in a new way our highs and lows of pain and pleasure. Once we open our hearts to the mystery of our true self, we fall in love with life all over again. We become men and women of good self-esteem.

To see the challenges of life as *splendid* is a step further in faith. It is a step that I take, as a Christian, in believing that the waterfalls of my life are not random, not meaningless, and not malignant. Rather, they become moments of trust, "free-fall moments" into the depths of the loving mystery of God, where I rediscover that God brings good out of all evil, victory out of all defeat, and resurrection out of death. Have I the faith to believe that the waters on the other side of this thundering fall will be as beautiful, as rich and peaceful as the river I am now so reluctant to leave? Do I have the faith to be open to that possibility, and to the opportunities for learning, that this thundering fall provides?

Notes

Chapter 1

1. A. Newberg and E. D'Aquili, *Brain Science and the Biology of Belief: Why God Won't Go Away*, New York: Ballantine Books, 2001, p. 13.
2. Quoted in H. Koenig, *The Healing Power of Faith: Science Explores Medicine's Last Great Frontier*, New York: Simon & Schuster, 1999, p. 246.
3. H. Benson, *Timeless Healing: The Power and the Biology of Belief*, New York: Scribner, 1996, p. 195.
4. L. Dossey, *Reinventing Medicine: Beyond Mind-Body to a New Era of Healing*, San Francisco: Harper & Row, 1999, p. 199.
5. Quoted by Newberg and D'Aquili, *Brain Science*, p. 129.
6. Interview in *The Scotsman*, November 13, 2001.
7. Quoted in V. Frankl, *The Unheard Cry for Meaning*, New York: Simon & Schuster, 1978, p. 34.
8. Ibid.
9. Koenig, *The Healing Power of Faith*, p. 222.
10. Ibid.
11. P. Scott Richards and A.E. Bergin, *Spiritual Strategy for Counseling and Psychotherapy*, Washington, DC: American Psychological Association, 1997, p. 80.
12. Ibid.
13. C. Saussy, *God Images and Self-Esteem*, Louisville: Westminster, 1991, p. 78.
14. T. S. Eliot, *Four Quartets*, London: Faber & Faber, 1944.

Chapter 2

1. N. Mandela, *Long Walk to Freedom*, London: Little, Brown, 1994, p. 376.
2. Ibid.
3. C. S. Lewis, *Fern-Seed and Elephants*, Glasgow: Fount, 1975, p. 40.
4. I. Yalom, *Love's Executioner and Other Tales of Psychotherapy*, London: Penguin, 1991.

Chapter 3

1. I should like to acknowledge the substantial contribution to the psychological content of this chapter made by Dr. Stephanie Thornton. The quotation is from C. H. Cooley, *Human Nature and the Social Order*, New York: Scribner's, 1902.
2. Cooley, *Human Nature and the Social Order*.
3. N. Branden, *How to Raise Your Self-Esteem*, New York: Bantam Books, 1987.
4. L. H. Ervin and S. Stryker, "Theorising the Relationship Between Self-Esteem and Identity," in T. Owens, S. Stryker, and N. Goodman (eds.), *Extending Self-Esteem Theory and Research: Sociological and Psychological Currents*, Cambridge, MA: Cambridge University Press, 2001.
5. M. Rosenberg and M. E. McCulloch, "Mattering: Inferred Significance and Mental Health among Adolescents," *Research in Community and Health*, vol. 2 (1981), pp. 163–182.
6. L. Pearlin and A. J. LeBlanc, "Bereavement and the Loss of Mattering," in Owens, Stryker, and Goodman (eds.), *Extending Self-Esteem Theory and Research*.
7. Quoted from Ronald Rolheiser, *Scottish Catholic Observer*, September 19, 2003.
8. V. Gecas, "The Self-Concept As a Social Force," in Owens, Stryker, and Goodman (eds.), *Extending Self-Esteem Theory and Research*.
9. John Paul II, *Redemptor Hominis*, para. 71.
10. Paul Wadell, *Friendship and the Moral Life*, Notre Dame, IN: Notre Dame Press, 1989, p. 158.
11. Second Vatican Council, *Gaudium et Spes*, para. 16.
12. H. Ward, *The Gift of Self*, London: Darton, Longman & Todd, 1990, p. 9.

Chapter 4

1. S. Coopersmith, *The Antecedents of Self-Esteem*, San Francisco: W.H. Freeman, 1967, p. 5.
2. G. Kaufman, *Shame: The Power of Caring*, Vermont: Schenkman Books, 1991, p. 102.
3. J. Gill, *Human Development*, no. 3 (1980), p. 34.
4. Coopersmith, *Antecedents of Self-Esteem*, p. 18.
5. B. Bettelheim, *A Good Enough Parent: A Guide to Bringing up Children*, London: Thames & Hudson, 1987.
6. T. Owens, S. Stryker, and N. Goodman (eds.), *Extending Self-Esteem Theory and Research: Sociological and Psychological Currents*, Cambridge, 2001.
7. J. Sacks, *The Dignity of Difference: How to Avoid the Clash of Civilizations*, London: Continuum, 2003, p. 47.
8. J. Sullivan, *Journey to Freedom*, New York: Paulist, 1987, p. 55.
9. M. Rosenberg and T. Owens, "Low Self-Esteem People: A Collective Portrait," in Owens, Stryker, and Goodman (eds.), *Extending Self-Esteem Theory and Research: Sociological and Psychological Currents*, Cambridge: Cambridge University Press, 2001.

Chapter 5

1. Paul Diemer, *Love Without Measure: Extracts From the Writings of St. Bernard of Clairvaux*, London: Darton, Longman & Todd, 1990, p. 15.
2. Charles Kirchberger (ed.), *Richard of St. Victor: Selected Writings on Contemplation*, London: Faber & Faber, 1995, p. 109.
3. Saint Teresa of Ávila, *The Interior Castle*, New York: Image Books, 1961, p. 37.
4. Catechism of the Catholic Church, para. 2340.
5. T. Owens, S. Stryker, and N. Goodman (eds.), *Extending Self-Esteem Theory and Research: Sociological and Psychological Currents*, Cambridge, MA: Cambridge University Press, 2001.
6. Wilkie Au and Noreen Cannon, "Perfectionism: A PseudoWholeness," in *Urgings of the Heart: A Spirituality of Integration*, New York: Paulist Press, 1995.
7. M. McKay and P. Fanning, *Self-Esteem: The Ultimate Self-Help Programme*, New York: MJF Books, 1992, p. 16.

8. Quoted in Leanne Payne, *Restoring the Christian Soul through Healing Prayer*, Eastbourne: Kingsway, 1992, p. 31.

9. Grace Davie, *Europe: The Exceptional Case*, London: Darton, Longman & Todd, 2002, p. 4.

Chapter 6

1. Fred Luskin, *Forgive for Good*, San Francisco: HarperCollins, 2002.

2. Sidney B. Simon and Suzanne Simon, *Forgiveness: How to Make Peace With Your Past and Get on With Your Life*, New York: Warner, 1991, p. 182.

3. Ibid., p. 182.

4. Ibid.

5. C. S. Lewis, *Letters to Malcolm: Chiefly on Prayer*, New York: Harcourt, Brace & World, 1964, p. 106.

6. Cf. Gregory Jones, *Embodying Forgiveness: A Theological Analysis*, Grand Rapids: Eerdmans, 1995, p. 177.

7. Philip C. McGraw, *Self Matters: Creating Your Life From the Inside Out*, London: Simon & Schuster, 2001, p. 282.

8. Robert Enright and Joanna North (eds.), *Exploring Forgiveness*, Madison, WI: University of Wisconsin Press, 1998, p. 47.

9. Jones, *Embodying Forgiveness*, p. 121.

10. Ibid., p. 230.

11. Simon Wiesenthal, *The Sunflower: On the Possibilities and Limits of Forgiveness*, New York: Schocken Books, 1988.

12. Gerald Jampolsky, *Forgiveness: The Greatest Healer of All*, Hillsboro, OR: Beyond Words, 1999, p. 17.

13. Enright and North (eds.), *Exploring Forgiveness*, p. 138.

14. Jampolsky, *Forgiveness*, p. 57.

15. Wiesenthal, *The Sunflower*, p. 130.

16. Enright and North (eds.), *Exploring Forgiveness*, p. 26.

17. Carl Jung, *Modern Man in Search of a Soul*, New York: A. Harvest/ HBJ Books, 1933, p. 235.

Chapter 7

1. Rudyard Kipling, "If," cited from *Oxford Dictionary of Quotations*, Oxford: Oxford University Press, 1985, p. 297.
2. Donald Gelpi, *Grace As Transmuted Experience and Social Process*, Lanham, Maryland: University Press of America, 1988, p. 102.
3. John Paul II, *Sollicitudo Rei Socialis* ("On Social Concerns"), para. 38.
4. John Paul II, *Novo Millennio Ineunte* ("At the Beginning of the New Millennium"), para. 52.
5. Ibid., para. 43.
6. Gelpi, *Grace As Transmuted Experience*.
7. For a clear presentation of Kohlberg's theory, see D. and S. Thornton, "Structure, Content and the Direction of Development in Kohlberg's Theory," in H. Weinreich-Haste and D. Locke (eds.), *Morality in the Making: Thought, Action and the Social Context*, Chichester: J. Wiley and Sons, 1983.
8. Carol Gilligan developed her critique in her classic, *In a Different Voice: Psychological Theory and Women's Development*, Cambridge, MA: Harvard University Press, 1982.
9. Bernard Lonergan, *Method in Theology*, London: Darton, Longman & Todd, 1973, p. 240.
10. Grace Davie, *Europe: The Exceptional Case*, London: Darton, Longman & Todd, 2002.
11. New Rite of Penance, para. 6.
12. Gelpi, *Grace As Transmuted Experience*, p. 111.

Permissions and Resources